*T*he moment you start "defining" something, it dies. It's dead. So I have nothing against any Christianity, Hinduism or Marxism—I have nothing against anyone or anything. But I do have something against—strongly AGAINST—anything that imprisons people. We've-got-the-truth syndrome, you know. It's in the bag once and for all, and that's it.

That's the falsehood I cannot stand.

The Truth is something that . . . "becomes." Something perpetually the same and forever in question, I could say, or in becoming. It isn't something you catch once and for all. It's something that . . . you must INCARNATE more and more.

To incarnate means to drive it into your own flesh.

And the point is, my whole search as a Sannyasi [errant monk] in India ended up in something that drove me OUT of my own flesh. That's where I was at the end of that whole search—at the end of what seemed to be the ULTIMATE search. Well, for me the ultimate wasn't ultimate. Or if that was ultimate, then I sympathize with the Buddhists, with the Illusionists, with those who throw bombs everywhere, for it's the active or negative way to reach the same end.

All those practices are nothing but a damn illusion.

We are offered a choice between getting out of it all and blowing everything up. On the one hand, yogis, Buddhists tell you, "The solution is Nirvana—go above"; and on the other hand, others tell you, "No, let's just bomb this whole damn world out of existence. . . ."

It's exactly the same thing.

One blissfully, the other diabolically, they are one and the same thing.

Two negations amounting to the same thing. Both roads are dead ends.

Or else this Earth has no sense.

This was the question bringing me back to Pondicherry, to . . . Her.

—*Satprem*

SATPREM was born in 1923 in Paris. At twenty, he was arrested by the Gestapo and spent one and a half year in concentration camps. Broken in his heart and body, he traveled to Egypt, then to India, where he served in the French government of Pondicherry. There he discovered the "new evolution" envisioned by Sri Aurobindo—"Man is a transitional being"—handed in his resignation and left for the Amazon jungle, ever in search of the "true adventure."

Upon his return to India in 1953, at the age of thirty, he became a mendicant Sannyasi, practiced Tantrism, finally to abandon all these paths to put himself at the service of Mother and Sri Aurobindo, to whom he dedicated his first nonfiction work, *Sri Aurobindo or the Adventure of Consciousness,* then a second nonfiction work, *On the Way to Supermanhood.* He stayed beside Mother for 19 years, becoming her confidant and witness, and recording numerous personal conversations that form *Mother's Agenda.* This adventure with her who was seeking the secret of the transition to the next species gave rise to a trilogy on Mother (*The Divine Materialism, The New Species, The Mutation of Death*), then to a fable, *Gringo,* and finally to *The Mind of the Cells,* his latest nonfiction work, which distills the essence of Mother's discovery: a change in the genetic program and a different view of death. Satprem now lives withdrawn from public life to devote himself to the transition in the consciousness of the body.

FRÉDÉRIC DE TOWARNICKI, a French journalist known for his in-depth interviews with the great philosophers and scientists of our time, visited Satprem in India, where these conversations were taped, from April 29 to May 5, 1980, and later broadcast on French radio. After briefly discussing his own life of search and adventure in the Amazon jungle, Africa and India, Satprem explains Mother's attempt to open the door to a next human species on earth—what it means in practical terms and why this is perhaps the most urgent question facing our species today.

ISBN 0-938710-15-X

*my
burning
heart*

ALSO BY SATPREM

Sri Aurobindo or
The Adventure of Consciousness (1984)
By the Body of the Earth (1978)

*

Mother:
1. *The Divine Materialism* (1986)
2. *The New Species* (1982)
3. *The Mutation of Death* (1987)

*

The Mind of the Cells (1982)
On the Way to Supermanhood (1986)
Life Without Death (1988)

Mother's Agenda
1951-1973
13 volumes

Recorded by Satprem in the course of numerous personal conversations with Mother, the complete logbook of her fabulous exploration in the cellular consciousness of the human body. Twenty-three years of experiences which parallel some of the most recent theories of modern physics. Perhaps the key to man's passage to the next species. (Vols. 1, 2, 3, 4, 5, 6, 12 & 13 published in English)

Satprem

my burning heart

INTERVIEW BY
F. DE TOWARNICKI

Translated from the French

Institute for Evolutionary Research
200 Park Avenue, New York, N.Y. 10166

For information address:
    Institute for Evolutionary Research
    200 Park Avenue, Suite 303 East
    New York, NY 10166

Library of Congress Cataloging-in-Publication Data

Satprem, 1923–
    My burning heart.

        Translation of: Sept jours en Inde avec Satprem.
            1. Satprem, 1923–   —Interviews. 2. Spiritual life
    (Hinduism). 3. Ghose, Aurobindo, 1872–1950. 4. Mother, 1878–
    1973. 5. Sri Aurobindo Ashram—
    Biography. I. Towarnicki, Frédéric de. II. Title.
    BL1175.S3855A3   1989   294.5'092 [B]   89-2141
    ISBN 0-938710-15-X

Manufactured in the United States of America

CONTENTS

A Sea Gull and Barbed Wire

The Journey

TOWARNICKI: *In tales of yore, one often heard such things as: "It was the end of the day. Someone was walking on a road when he happened upon a very old man. Then morning came . . ." And at the end of the tale something was conveyed.*

So, Satprem, I would like you sometimes to tell this tale as a saga, or a chanson de geste, and at other times as the expression of a thought process, which would allow me to ask you questions such as "What is the meaning of hyperconsciousness, of matter? How did they come about? . . ."

Yours is therefore a spiritual journey. . . .

SATPREM: Well, primarily I . . . What's interesting to me is primarily Mother. What she did. What was done.

TOWARNICKI: *Yes, but before you met her . . .*

Yes, there's a whole course.

TOWARNICKI: *There were several stages before that meeting?*

Yes.

TOWARNICKI: *First, there was that question. And the entire journey is a gradual and more and more complete answer to that first question, until . . . But before meeting Mother, there were the camps, the jungle, the roads of India, Tantrism. . . . Satprem, what were the stages, the landmarks of that adventure, of that journey?*

Oh, my first stage was the seashore: a child looking out into space.

That's the beginning, and perhaps the end, of everything.

But I've seen a lot. I've gone through a lot of experiences from my childhood in Brittany to the concentration camps and then to India. . . . Well, actually, first to Egypt.

From Egypt I went to India, and that's where I discovered Sri Aurobindo and Mother—their gaze.

Then I left, this time on an adventure to French Guiana, in the jungle, then on to Brazil, Africa. Then back to India, because that gaze had struck me. Mother was there.

Once again I took to the road. I became a sannyasi [monk], wandering through Ceylon, India, the Himalayas. And finally I came back—this time for nineteen years—to Pondicherry, to Mother, for that exploration of the body, of the cells, of the next species: what is COMING, what we are in the process of becoming, each and everyone of us, however unaware of it we may be.

> TOWARNICKI: *You had your own quest, then, before meeting Sri Aurobindo and Mother. If you don't mind, let us begin with that quest, which lasted more than ten years in the earth's past. That's how it all began, before meeting Sri Aurobindo.*

Well, actually, he is the one who determined my quest.

> TOWARNICKI: *Oh, right from the start?*

Yes. He is the one who gave meaning to my quest.
But quest for what? Words are all so abstract.
Quest for what? What does a man really search for?

> TOWARNICKI: *Well, in a spiritual journey, one can speak of a "quest," no?*

Yes, a quest, but . . . These are abstract words, you see.
Quest for what? What does a man actually search for?
When does the question begin?
One formulates it in one's mind at fifteen or twenty, but it's already there much earlier.

A Childhood in Brittany

When a child opens his eyes, he is always like the first human being in the world. And he says to himself, "What?" (without any words, of course; he IS a question). Man WAS a question. We thought we had to provide mental, intellectual answers to the question. But even after we provide all

3

the answers, they still will not fulfill anything. For the question is about BEING.

As far back as I can remember, I see a child, on the seashore, gazing out. . . . Gazing at what? I don't know, but gazing. His gaze is already a question. And our whole life is made of that very same thing which was there at the beginning, when we were looking at the little wave on the beach. It's that same . . . yearning TOWARD something. And there comes a moment in life when that yearning is satisfied, fulfilled.

TOWARNICKI: *You were in Brittany when you gazed at that little beach?*

Oh, yes! That's where I spent my childhood. I lived by the sea. And in fact, I only felt comfortable when I was on a boat. Whenever I was at sea, I had the feeling of everything vanishing, of there being only the waves, the wind, and no longer any "me" at all—the feeling of being spread out everywhere, as it were, lost in an expanse of light. And it was very pleasant. But the moment I returned to land, it suddenly felt like returning to a prison. I had no idea why, of course; I just felt terrible. Returning to land was the moment when things started to feel terrible.

TOWARNICKI: *You were a sailor?*

Well, I was a kid. . . . I was a sailor boy! I went out sailing. I went out on the sea.

I had a little cockleshell of a boat and I would go as far as I possibly could—as rashly as I could. And I felt very good as long as there was vastness, space and "nobody." Then, the minute I came back to shore, everything started to grate.

And that's just when . . . that may be when the question began: on the one hand, that state I could not explain, of feeling so happy at sea with the wind, the sky and space; and the minute I was back on land, I felt miserable. That's perhaps how it all began.

For me there was therefore a state of fulness and a state of want—which eventually grew into an increasingly distressing absence. Not distressing—oppressing.

TOWARNICKI: *One day you said you suffocated a little when you were on land.*

I spent my time suffocating on land! I spent, I don't know, twenty years of my life suffocating. Until—

TOWARNICKI: *—Why?*

Because I found that world suffocating. Family, friends, education—it all seemed so very small, so narrow. You can't breathe freely; everything grates. And the only plenitude I knew was physical—and I don't even know about "plenitude," because it's just another word, but it was a moment when there was no longer any "I," no longer any words. I just felt at ease with myself when I was on the open sea, and I felt terrible when I was on land.

The trouble is, you can't spend all your time on a boat!

TOWARNICKI: *You might be taken to task for refusing to put up with the constraints of everyday life, which everybody has to face: teachers, school, discipline. . . .*

I found all that absolutely unbearable.

I found it absolutely FALSE. Well, I am again putting a value on it: it's "false" because what is good and true should be able to be breathed easily.

Every quest for—we use abstract words, but what, after all, is truth? It is what feels good and can be breathed easily. It has nothing to do with metaphysics, you know.

Well, the only life I knew—which, I think, is the life of any young Westerner—felt suffocating to me. All the education they drum into you—Latin declensions, Greek verbs, boarding school. They stuck me into one boarding school after another because I was insufferable. I was an absolute nuisance! So I was put into one boarding school, then a second one, then a third one, and everything seemed . . . dreadful to me. I couldn't bear even my family.

Looking back on all that, one might say: Well, that's "growing pains." People give all sorts of so-called psychological explanations. But there is only one thing: a WANT . . . the child feels a WANT of something. And every human being, whether he is aware of it or not, feels a WANT of something, which he clumsily tries to fill with one thing or another, and then another. But it never gets filled. And in my case, what was missing was missing in an excruciating way. Why, I don't know. But it was a fact.

TOWARNICKI: *At the time, you didn't know what was missing.*

I didn't have the faintest idea.

TOWARNICKI: *It was already the beginning of a question?*

It was *the* question.

The pity is that people don't quite know how to trace the origin of their question, the first occurrence of their question. So they make up all sorts of false questions. They give all sorts of false answers to try somehow to fill that . . . void, that want, that absence.

TOWARNICKI: *But they become aware of this only much later, no?*

Yes. . . . They are also satisfied with very little.

That's what makes the difference between humans; it isn't a question of intelligence, of this or that quality. The difference lies in the "intensity" of need or the intensity of want.

That's what makes the difference between humans beings.

(short silence)

Some people are really like human babies. Their needs are utterly material, and if there are enough noise and friends and books around them, they are content. Well, those are the human babies. There are plenty of them.

Others are more questioning, if I may say, or have more difficulty breathing.

And the great pity is that those for whom the question is really like a need to breathe freely don't have much to satisfy their question, to fill that hole—because, in fact, it is a hole. It's a hole, something that's . . . terribly missing.

TOWARNICKI: *People feel uneasy, miserable?*

Yes, increasingly so. Actually, that's the marvel of our twentieth century; there has never been a more marvelous period in history! Because we are really beginning to come to the real question, and to the need for a real answer. While only twenty-five years ago, people were full of political, economic, metaphysical illusions—they ranted and raved about all that stuff as if everything would eventually turn out right.

Well, now it's marvelous; we no longer have the illusion that everything is going to be all right. We are coming to the real question. And hence to the real answer, because it's the same thing. The "question" is itself the answer. To ask the question in the true way—there are not a hundred ways of asking it: you ask with your heart, with your breath—to ask it in the true way, that is, to incarnate it, to BE it in the true way, is already the answer.

It's already the answer.

TOWARNICKI: *Can one express the question, though?*

I think that . . . expressing it is precisely what's wrong.

TOWARNICKI: *For most people it's "What is life? Why do I live? . . ."*

Yes, it's always—

TOWARNICKI: —*"How should I live?"*

Yes, one always immediately looks for a mental answer. But what we actually need is an answer of a different order, something that has nothing to do with morality, philosophy, religion and all that. Each of these human approaches tries to give an answer or a satisfaction; and each, in the course of a person's development, may bring something. But it isn't something that can really fulfill you. It can't.

TOWARNICKI: *Perhaps we needn't be too specific, but sometimes the place is relevant—your Breton origin, for instance. Satprem is Breton. It may be in Brittany that, as a child, the very first question arose in him, without any answer. Today we are in the blue mountains of South India. If I say, "Satprem, you are Breton," does it still mean something for you?*

Oh, certainly! The sea has a deep echo in me—as the place where everything began for me. I so often feel that, whatever I may have found today, at fifty-seven, I used to live it, breathe it when I was six or seven years old. And I lived it there, in Brittany.

TOWARNICKI: *Where?*

On the sea—oh, you mean where geographically? Is it necessary to be specific?

All I can say is that it was not too far from Belle-Ile.

So, yes, my origin means something very physical for me. . . . But in fact, for me, truth is physical, it's as simple as that. I can feel it only when it throbs in my body.

The state of truth, for me, is a state in which the BODY is in harmony, feels unconfined. A sense of . . . freedom from all boundaries. Then you know: this is true. Everything else is just passing thoughts; it's hardly interesting at all. What is needed is to live THAT constantly, to be constantly in the state of truth, that is, the state of harmony, of plenitude. And people won't be satisfied as long as that state of truth has not become as simple as breathing air.

I really wonder how . . . All this Western way of life in particular gives me such a feeling of ENORMOUS artificiality. I am not just talking about the machinery but about the way people live: with books, thoughts, with a dash of aesthetics thrown in; in other words, how they more or less successfully fill their life. To me, even at its best, it seems so artificial. I repeat: even at its best—when they look at a beautiful painting or listen to a beautiful piece of music (although music *can* break limits). But all that is momentary, you see. It isn't the deep, full breathing of human beings. They live like automatons for 23 hours and 50 minutes, and perhaps for only 10 minutes a day something happens—and sometimes, not even that.

Well, the minute I felt that lack of truth, as it were—that is, when I returned to land and met with conflicts, people— the minute I felt that lack of truth, something in me became ABSOLUTELY steadfast in the need to experience that breathing in a total way. Not just for a minute, not just for an hour while I was at sea—to experience it CONSTANTLY.

And why couldn't I experience it on land?

So that's what drove me this way and that for years, what made me search in every direction, for every . . . well, not remedies, but perhaps for escapes, too.

TOWARNICKI: *The sea, in other words, was your first object lesson?*

Oh, indeed!

TOWARNICKI: *As a child?*

Yes, yes—the sea, space.

Religious Education: Walls

TOWARNICKI: *I wanted to ask you this: Were you reading at the time? And what were you reading? There was surely the Bible! There was surely the Breton religious atmosphere! There was surely Sunday services, the priest! Can I ask that question?*

Yes, certainly you can.

TOWARNICKI: *All right. Who, then, is the child Satprem? What does he read? Is he an illiterate child? (laughter) Actually, perhaps it was not "the child Satprem." . . .*

Yes, it was probably Satprem.

TOWARNICKI: *All right. Who was the child Satprem? Did he go to church? Did he have a religious education?*

Oh, I couldn't stand it. . . . Yes, of course, I had a religious education. My father was a very religious man—thanks to him, I was disgusted with religion once and for all.
I felt imprisoned.

TOWARNICKI: *Even in church?*

Rather in my father's attitude—and hence in church. I felt they were trying to put something over me. And all my life, from a very young age, I have never been able to stand the feeling of being imprisoned by something.
It was a reaction . . . in my very chromosomes (I don't know where it was, but . . .) To feel imprisoned was unbearable. I couldn't stand that religious influence in my father, in my

11

family (they sent me to a Jesuit school), and I hated religion. I hated anything that confines you.

A church meant a building. And, for me, to go and sit in a building was the first lie. I felt life when there were no walls, you see; then a certain rhythm settled in me in which I felt at ease. So those walls—it could as well have been a temple, a mosque or anything, but to me they were all the same!

For me, anything that had to be put inside four walls was the first step toward falsehood, or suffocation. That's all.

The Camps

TOWARNICKI: *And then there were the camps.*

Oh, yes. . . . That was a brutal grace dealt to me. Precisely because I had such a need of . . . of truth—"truth," well, I don't know what word to use. Or, let's say, a need to BE. Yes, a need to be.

Because of that need, I think I was given the grace—brutally—to begin to touch a real answer!

TOWARNICKI: *The concentration camps made you touch the heart of certain things?*

Oh, in a sense they helped me wonderfully—by shattering all human values in me. Everything was torn to pieces, devastated. And not only by what I saw, but by what I went through myself. I was just . . . twenty, you see, just twenty when I went there.

TOWARNICKI: *How did it happen, Satprem? You were arrested by the Gestapo because you were a member of the French Resistance?*

I was arrested by the Gestapo.

Yes, without warning. We had been betrayed. There was a man from the German counterespionage in our ranks and we didn't know it. So I was on a mission, because we had just learned of that man's betrayal, and I had gone to warn some of our comrades or agents. But the very one I was warning was also a traitor! I had gone to tell him, "Be careful, we've been betrayed," and that man was also a traitor! So as soon as I left his house, he telephoned the Gestapo. And I was barely five hundred feet from his house, about to take a streetcar, when a car from the *Kriminal Polizei* came to a screeching halt in front of me. Two men came out, pistols in hand, and arrested me on the spot.

Well, it was rather like in the movies, you know. But . . .

TOWARNICKI: *Where did they take you?*

They took me to prison. And then it began.

Those are not things that . . . They are not things one should talk about.

At any rate, all that broke . . . broke me, CLEANSED me wonderfully—dreadfully, but wonderfully. Because how many years would I have spent getting rid of all the social, familial, intellectual, cultural clothing—everything that had been heaped on me for twenty years?

Well, everything that had been heaped on me was shattered, me included (what I thought was me).

There was nothing left of me.

But this is the point: what I thought was me.

I thought it was a lot of music, poetry, this and that. And it was all suddenly shattered. All that was left was a sort of human residue, suddenly face to face with death, fear, the horrible human wretchedness, and saying to itself, "But

13

what . . . what . . . what is this?" You see, at that moment in life, there are no more barriers between the man who abuses and the one who is being abused. There are no more a "man from the Gestapo" and a "victim of the Gestapo," an SS man and a prisoner—just a sort of horror in which you are plunged. There aren't "others," you see. You are . . . totally immersed in horror. The horror is not others; it's something within which you are.

So everything I might have been, everything I thought I was was so radically shattered that I was suddenly thrust into . . . well, into the only thing left: my own flesh.

Yes, all of sudden, I felt a fantastic joy. All of a sudden, I was as if above it all, almost "laughing." As if, all at once, I came out of that devastation into a place that was . . . "royal." I was no longer a prisoner, I was no longer assaulted, I was no longer . . . I was above, looking at all that with . . . almost with laughter.

And suddenly it was like being that kid on the sea again, on his boat, feeling like a king.

> **Towarnicki:** *One day you wrote, "I asked myself what is left in a man when nothing is left?"*

Yes.

> **Towarnicki:** *That's the depth you touched?*

Yes! And just when there is nothing left, well, there is suddenly "something" that's literally bursting with plenitude.

When I began to formulate questions, I suppose around the age of fourteen, I used to say to myself, "Let's see: remove your father, remove your mother, remove friends, remove books, remove music—what's left of you? What is YOU in this body which is not your father, your mother, boarding school, friends, etc? Where is YOU?"

That's a question I asked very often, when I began to formulate things.

What is YOU?

I asked it when I was on land. At sea there were no questions. But on land, yes: where is "you"?

And then . . . when I was sixteen or seventeen, I dreamed of a sort of "life of adventure" where you are like an unknown chemical element: you create reactions within yourself. You mix in all sorts of chemical reagents to discover your composition.

And I imagined that my life should be like a chemical experiment in which the fellow who was supposedly "me" would be forced to SPIT OUT his truth, to GIVE OFF his truth, to RING with his true "sound."

TOWARNICKI: *To test himself?*

Yes, to find out what's in there. That was my question. My only question.

And perhaps it is because I had that intense a question that I was soon given a response.

At twenty—twenty years and fifteen days—I started to be given the response. By being stripped of everything that had been put on me. And what was left was: what's-left-when-nothing-is-left.

TOWARNICKI: *Were you struck by any particular incident involving the SS or the guards of the camp that would indicate that forces other than horror may sometimes be at work in the worst moments of life?*

15

You mean in life or . . .?

TOWARNICKI: *I mean an incident in the camps that might have shown you that "evil" was not all powerful.*

I don't know.

(silence)

TOWARNICKI: *Well, I mean, in the midst of that horror of the camps, that machinery of the camps, sometimes there may happen . . . Do you remember what happened on the edge of the Auroville canyons, for example?[1] Certain events may have struck you, may have shown you that, sometimes, Moloch is vulnerable! It happens. An intimate recognition that all those people guarding you were in the end only straw men? Do you have a recollection about an inmate's behavior, something that might have shown you that that ruthless force itself had weaknesses?*

Oh, it was too absolute! . . . It was too absolute.

There are no weaknesses in a nightmare. You just have to get out of the nightmare.

I really can't say. I have no special recollection of any bright spot in all that, except when, in the midst of that frightful nullity, I suddenly emerged into an inexpressible joy . . . (I can't explain; I don't know what word to use, because it isn't "joy"). All of a sudden, I emerged into something that was extraordinarily pure and strong—STRONG,

---

1. When Satprem was attacked by a group of thugs determined to take his life and was "miraculously" able to escape their grasp unharmed.

you know. STRONG—nothing could touch me anymore.

TOWARNICKI: *A sense of serenity, perhaps?*

Oh, no! . . . Serenity . . . Certainly not serenity!
A force—a force, you understand. Something that made
me suddenly invulnerable. And nothing could harm me.

That was my first contact with . . . (how I understand
now!), the first contact with the truth, with what one IS—
what every human being IS, in fact, because when you touch
that core of BEING, you touch what is everywhere. Whether
it's another person, a plant or an animal, you are in touch
with the very being of the world. And the very being of the
world is something that's full, powerful and . . . "regal."

That's the only thing I felt in the camps. Other than that,
I don't see any moments of grace. Except once, maybe (I'm
sure it was done intentionally). . . . There were some bomb-
ings and we had been crammed into a tunnel. Some civilians
were there, and one of them left a package of margarine or
something like that behind for us. And I knew it had been
done intentionally. For a minute I thought, "Well, there's
. . . well, that's something."

That's all.

But otherwise there weren't too many graces.

TOWARNICKI: *And of course, it's only much later that you
were able to understand the meaning of that force?*

On that occasion I began to touch a certain way of breathing.

I mean, when I was a child I could feel those vast and
luminous things, and one breathes easily. But there I felt it
as a force. It was more like a force that I touched upon. It

expressed itself as a force, and it took me a long time to understand what it was.

And afterwards you have only one thought—only one thought: may what came once be there ALL THE TIME .

Your only thought is to find the secret or the mechanism of that minute, when it was suddenly so absolute and invincible. You want to understand it—not just understand; you want to TOUCH it again.

First Trip to India: Sri Aurobindo's Gaze

TOWARNICKI: *Now you've left the camps. And the question is still there?*

Well, I don't know. For me, the period after the camps may have been more dreadful than during the camps.

I had a few very difficult years, wondering whether I was going to be able to survive or not. Because, you see, that minute, those minutes—or few weeks or months, I don't know—when I felt that force HOLDING me, had left me, when I came out of the camps. When I came out, it was gone. I found myself back in everyday life, but I was a devastated man. So how do you hold up then?

For a long, long time, I had spells of disgust, very destructive urges.

TOWARNICKI: *Nausea?*

It was worse than nausea; it was like a shattered life. What was there to look for? What could the West offer me?

I had enrolled at Ecole Coloniale because I kept thinking that adventure was to be found in the colonies, primarily because they were so far away. But I found myself dealing with school programs and fellow students. . . . It's as if I had landed from another planet among all those people who seemed so confident about their life . . . for whom life was so natural! While, for me, nothing was natural anymore.

Once, I remember, something had deeply struck me.

It was the first time I was taken in a police van from the prison in Fresnes to rue des Saussaies,[1] where we were interrogated. And the police van followed a certain route. It passed very close to where I used to live, in the Latin Quarter. Down the street . . . then Boulevard Raspail . . . right there. Suddenly, in the moving police van, through the grille, I saw that street—the very street where I used to go walking. I saw the housewives with their baskets going to get bread at the bakery, and all of a sudden it all looked so FRIGHTENING to me, you know, that place where I lived . . . those women with their baskets going to get bread. . . . It all looked . . . nothing had reality anymore! It was frightening.

I can't explain.

That was one of the most powerful moments of my life.

It was as if the reality of the world as I knew it had been destroyed.

TOWARNICKI: *Things had lost their reality for you?*

It was . . . I was on the side of the dead! I don't know. Or on another side.

I was on another side.

From that minute on, life could no longer be natural, as people understand "natural." One could no longer go with a basket and get bread, you know.

And that's the state I was in when I came out of the camps. I was truly on another planet, and it was . . . unbearable.

---

1. A Gestapo headquarters in German-occupied Paris.

TOWARNICKI: *You had enrolled at Ecole Coloniale?*

Yes.

TOWARNICKI: *In what city?*

In Paris.

TOWARNICKI: *In Paris?*

I was still in that contradiction: I was half-Breton, half-Parisian. In other words, I had one foot on the open sea and one foot in prison. It was exactly like that!

But there again, a grace came knocking on my door.

I had a cousin who had just been appointed governor of Pondicherry, in French India, and he said to me, "How would you like to come with me to India?" It was my salvation, because I really don't know what I would have done in Paris. It was my salvation. He took me along with him. . . . And I saw Sri Aurobindo.

And the day I saw Sri Aurobindo, all of a sudden . . . well, I was filled by that same thing I had . . . gropingly experienced as a child, that I had touched in the camps.

And it was RIGHT THERE. It was looking at me and filling me—right in front of me.

It was in front of me, alive. It was right there, in a gaze.

TOWARNICKI: *Try to remember. Tell me about that meeting. How does one meet, in India, a man like Sri Aurobindo?*

With Sri Aurobindo it was a little special. He never received anybody. But three or four times a year, his disciples, and whoever wished to, were allowed to pass in front of him to see him (what is called a "darshan" in India).

So that day, I followed the crowd and passed in front of him, thinking he was a great thinker, you see, and that's all. Sri Aurobindo was a "thinker," a "philosopher." Through the little I had read of him on arrival, to acquaint myself, I thought he was a great thinker.

And it wasn't a thinker that I met; it was a gaze—it was a being that I met.

TOWARNICKI: *But where was he?*

He was seated in a big armchair, with Mother beside him. And there was a sort of procession—actually, you passed before him in order to be LOOKED AT by him. Not to look at him, but in order for his gaze to open up . . . that door in us, the door that fills.

TOWARNICKI: *Did you already know his work?*

No. But as soon as I arrived in India, before meeting him, I immediately read *Essays on the Gita*; I read a number of books. . . . And immediately I felt: this isn't like anything you've ever read before, not like anything you've understood before. It's something different.

But to me he was still a "thinker." And suddenly, I was before something that was not a "thinker," before a being unlike any I had met on earth. A being who was a BEING, living. Not a man in a three-piece suit, or even with a white *chaddar* on his back. Something that was . . . that embodied in a gaze, in a body, in his atmosphere, what I had experienced on the open sea, in my boat. That whole immensity was there, in a being. And IT was looking at me.

21

So it's as if I suddenly recognized my home. I recognized the place where I could breathe, the place I came from—I was home.

TOWARNICKI: *And it all happened in the flash of a look?*

It lasted, I don't know, four seconds. . . . Four seconds. And I never forgot it.

TOWARNICKI: *As when Swami Vivekananda met Rama-krishna for the first time. It lasted a fraction of a second.*

It's a recognition, you see. That's exactly it. It isn't that you discover something different; you suddenly recognize something.
It's . . . like a "yes," but so much deeper than a "yes." That is "IT," you see. It's no longer a stranger. It's me looking at myself—it's ME, suddenly. Me, really me, precisely the what's-left after it has been stripped of all its falsehood and superfluity. The what's-left.
That's what was in those eyes.

TOWARNICKI: *It was your first meeting.*

Yes. I never forgot it.
So I decided I had to live that. I said to myself: If one man can embody that, can BE that, which I felt as being "mine," well, that's what I must live, what I must find.
But I wasn't yet . . . I still had a lot of journeying to do.
And to begin with, it was in an ashram—an ashram was just another church and I couldn't take that. Walls and me . . . all walls were a prison for me. Whether they were of the

Orient or the West didn't make any difference. So joining the "Sri Aurobindo Ashram" was out of the question. Absolutely out of the question!

But . . . that gaze kept pursuing me. That being, that minute of being kept pursuing me.

I left.

That gaze made me decide to . . . break once and for all with that pseudo-future I had planned for myself in the colonial administration. So I said to myself, "I'm through with this. I can't bear it anymore." I can't pretend to live. It isn't possible anymore.

I handed in my resignation from that colonial "career." And I left.

Landing in Cayenne

TOWARNICKI: *But you left for where?*

First, I went back to Paris. Once there, I had no idea what to do. Then, one day, while walking down a street, I passed a travel agency displaying a sort of world map in its window, with shipping lines marked in red. So I said to myself, "This line." At the other end of the line was written "Cayenne." I said to myself, "Cayenne is where I'm going."

And I was delighted! I thought, "This must be hell, for sure! So let's go there. Let's go to hell. Let's go right to the bottom of hell and find out what's in it."

Because, in my romantic imagination, Cayenne stood for all sorts of hellish things. . . .[1] I thought, "I'll go there, right in the depths of hell, and I'll experience the same thing I experienced in the camps. I just want to BE THAT."

---

1. Until 1945 Cayenne was the center of French penal settlements.

So I took a steerage ticket, and I went to Cayenne. Just like that.

TOWARNICKI: *To do what?*

Oh, I had no idea! Anything! Just to . . . go to hell—to hell, if possible, or anything—but to the BOTTOM of it all, to the END—to THE Thing.

To the place where this flesh, this being, had to CRY OUT its being. Or else die.

I wasn't attached to life. I was attached to . . . well, if I must die, let me die while going to the extreme limit.

And that's where I discovered something marvelous.

What is so marvelous when there is a real question in a being is that all sorts of answers start coming. Every grace (we can call it what we like), every grace comes to help him.

When I look at my whole course—painful, so painful—in which I went through so many things, I always, always see the hand of the grace helping me—helping here, there, everywhere, and answering my call. That's the point! If only people knew. . . . They complain about their existence, but it's because they aren't sincere.

Because there is a certain sincerity of call that elicits an INEVITABLE and material response—MATERIAL, you understand.

TOWARNICKI: *It isn't an answer in the beyond.*

Absolutely not! I don't believe in that at all.

It's an answer in matter.

I roamed through Guiana with *The Life Divine* as my only baggage. And in my Parisian shoes. That's how I arrived in the jungle.

TOWARNICKI: *The book by Sri Aurobindo?*

Yes, *The Life Divine*. I had it in one hand and my Parisian shoes on my feet, and that's all. That's how I went into the jungle.

> **TOWARNICKI:** *What you have called "a meeting with the earth's past"?*

Yes.
But I still had some difficult times there.
Because it's all very well: you arrive in the forest with your Parisian shoes, but, suddenly, you are face to face with such an element . . . For several days I was . . . (how to put it?), I wouldn't say "afraid," because I had gone through enough things in my life not to be afraid anymore, but . . . I just didn't realize what the jungle was!
I had a few days that were a bit . . . physically frightening, when I didn't know . . . I didn't know how to live anymore.

> **TOWARNICKI:** *But, Satprem, you reach Cayenne, right?*

Yes.

> **TOWARNICKI:** *Don't tell me you rush off into the jungle!*

(laughter) No, no! This is how it happened. . . .

> **TOWARNICKI:** *Yes, how? How does one do it?*

On the ship, in steerage, I had met a fellow who was a "mineral hunter" and who said to me, "There's a Mining Office in Cayenne. So if you want to go into the forest (because that's where I was headed, of course), if you want to go into the forest, you can start through the Mining Office, by offering your services as a prospector or whatever they will take."

So that's where I immediately went on arrival—I had no money, nothing whatsoever, you see. I went to the Mining Office and said, "I want to go into the forest, and I'm ready to do anything!"

And I was taken to—

TOWARNICKI: *Did they warn you? Did they say, "It's difficult"?*

Oh, not at all! Actually, that man must have understood a few things—he caught on right away.

I was put in a rowboat with some West Indians and I started out; together with another European, I began the apprenticeship of the jungle.

And that's where I had a few difficult days. . . . Much as in the camps, where I had been humanly broken, there, during the first days in the forest, it was also a physical ordeal: Suddenly I was . . . at once overwhelmed and a bit like a drowning man. When you find yourself in that . . . You have no idea what the jungle can be!

TOWARNICKI: *Yes* . . .

It's a teeming, awesome, frightening world. It's full of snakes. Lots of snakes.

At the beginning that's what made me . . . You can't walk three feet without meeting one. There are really lots of snakes there.

But it's such a . . . fantastic world!

So, for a few days, I felt as if completely uprooted from my body. I hardly knew where I was physically. Then, all of a sudden, a sort of understanding took place between that forest and me.

And there I lived some . . . I spent a whole year deep in the jungle.

TOWARNICKI: *Almost on your own?*

At the beginning there were two other people. Afterwards, I went on my own with a friend. Well, we . . .

> **TOWARNICKI:** *Tell me what it means to spend a day and a night deep in the jungle, in contact with the power of the earth. . . . Or next time?*

Maybe. . . .

The Bowels of the Devil

Cayenne: The Jungle

TOWARNICKI: *And then . . .*

SATPREM: Yes, for me Cayenne was a "challenge" rather than a choice.

TOWARNICKI: *A challenge?*

A challenge.

TOWARNICKI: *To what?*

Probably because it was . . . Cayenne has a whole history as a penitentiary, as an accursed place.

To begin with, you land on Devil's Island! *(laughter)* That was perfect for me! I thought, "All right, let's go and see what the bowels of the devil are all about!"

And then . . . in steerage I had met a prospector headed for Guiana, who said to me, "Listen, there's a Mining Office in Cayenne. You can try to get them to hire you. They're looking for . . . It's rather difficult to find people willing to go into the jungle. So they'll be glad to take you."

So I went to see the man at the Mining Office, and he took me on immediately. I was put in a rowboat with some West Indians, and off I went for my first lesson in the jungle.

And I must say it was . . . Landing in that jungle was like entering a . . . cataclysm.

For a few days I was . . . as if outside of myself, torn out of myself, OVERWHELMED by a world so much . . . beyond measure with myself. A swarming, hissing, strident world. Gigantic trees, swamps, rain and rain and rain. I felt completely lost—more than lost; it was like entering a cataclysm. All the while with my *Life Divine* under my arm. And then what?

People don't realize. They spend their life with a particular suit of clothes on their back. And those clothes comprise a certain number of feelings, ideas, principles. There are all sorts of little things turning round and round in those clothes. Anyhow, they spend their life with a particular suit of clothes.

And suddenly the clothes are being torn off you.

But that's just what I wanted! Ever since I was a child in Brittany I always had the feeling that there was a secret to be found. Something had to be WRESTED from one's depths.

When I looked out at the sea, there was a big tree (what is it called? it's a sort of pine tree; it was just next to my bedroom window . . .). Cypress! There was a big, black cypress next to my bedroom window on the seashore. And I used to spend hours looking through that window.

And then there was a web . . . That day, I remember, there was a spider web hanging among the branches of the cypress. I was looking at that web. And suddenly, it's as if I were in the web. I saw myself . . . I saw that little fellow in the center of the web, with all the threads—which were primarily all the books I read, because I read tons of books, and then friends, relatives, family, the Jesuit boarding school, math, chemistry, and everything I was being taught. I really saw myself as if . . . caught in a web. And I thought, "What would happen if I cut all those threads?"

It was my recurring question: "If I cut all the threads, maybe I would get to the secret?" I felt there was a secret. A life is a secret—each thing in it. We have to WREST a secret out of ourselves. And everything is a sort of pretext to wrest out what is there, in the depths of this human flesh.

When I was at sea, on my boat, those clothes, well, were cast off. And I merged with something that was extremely satisfying, luminous, vast, light. There was no more . . . weight anywhere.

And then, brutally, I found that again in the concentration camps: all of a sudden the clothes were torn off; there was nothing left—there was nothing left, yet there was suddenly something.

Then, again, in Sri Aurobindo's gaze: all of a sudden the clothes were torn off. And . . . something else was there.

I wanted to grasp hold of that secret, you understand.

For me, life was a SECRET to be found.

And in the middle of that forest, the same thing: all of a sudden, everything was so overwhelming, at once so beautiful and frightening. For despite everything I had gone through, I was still a good little middle-class Western boy. Despite everything, I had a very French education. And there I was, in the middle of that cataclysm.

TOWARNICKI: *Can you describe that feeling in the forest?*

You are overwhelmed in every way.

Those gigantic trees, so beautiful, so extraordinary! Those creeping lianas everywhere. That hissing . . . that constant hissing, those sounds, those swamps—you can't take three steps without walking into a swamp. Sometimes it's as silent as death, and suddenly it's teeming. And snakes everywhere. That was the main thing in the beginning— snakes. It was . . . I really felt uneasy, because they're completely invisible.

And the West Indians . . . There were two West Indian porters making fun of me. They had perfectly understood I had landed in the forest fresh from Paris, and they were having a good time. They wanted to put me to the test—and put me to the test they did.

TOWARNICKI: *How?*

Oh, in lots of ways. With snakes, in particular.

The thing is, you couldn't see those snakes! And they are everywhere, you see. They blend so perfectly with the landscape. You're just about to put your foot on one, and at the very last second you step over it. . . . You put your hand on a branch, and there's one right there. There are truly lots of snakes in that forest. Other than that, it's rather empty, except for snakes.

So I was rather in a state of, I don't know, like a shipwrecked man, I could say, for a number of . . . for about three or four days.

TOWARNICKI: *Somewhere you speak of the vibration of the forest.*

It's a swarming, hissing, vibrating world. It isn't a human world! It's really like entering another world. And this is why you suddenly feel "shipwrecked"—you must adjust to that, the body must become ATTUNED to all that.

And then one day, after two or three days (I even had a fever one night, it was so STRONG; that forest was so powerful, so overpowering), I had a fever because I couldn't . . . I couldn't get into it! I was still in my Western skin, you see.

My clothes were being torn off me. I was struggling with something I couldn't fathom. I got a fever because of it.

The day after the fever, it was all over. Suddenly I said to myself, "Look, why do you react this way? Are you afraid of dying?"

And so (laughter), I suddenly laughed and said, "Well, if I put my foot on a snake, I'll put my foot on a snake! If I put my hand on a snake, I'll put my hand on a snake! AND I DON'T GIVE A DAMN!"

And the moment that "I don't give a damn" came out of my heart, of my "guts," it was all over! There was a MARVELOUS communion with everything. I no longer looked where I walked. I didn't pay attention to anything. I only concerned myself with LOVING, and being with that forest and throwing myself into its arms. And it was marvelous.

And I couldn't possibly set foot on a snake anymore! Nothing could touch me! No mishap was possible! I . . . I flowed with the forest. I was in its music, its frenzy; I was in its brutal beauty, in its silence. . . . I flowed with it all.

TOWARNICKI: *But one day you said or wrote, "What one learns, too, is that man is but a speck in the universe."*

Oh, yes, that's very true.
Yes, he's a minuscule speck.

First, you disappear in it! After you've managed to give out that sort of cry: "I don't care; I don't care about anything! I'm taking the plunge, I'll lose myself there," the way you throw yourself into the sea—it's an element: you literally throw yourself into the forest. From that moment on, well, even the speck had disappeared! There only remained something that joyfully mingled with it all, with the life of the trees, the water, the rain, the sounds. . . . It was a kind of wonder. And then, sometimes . . . yes, at night, at night. . .

The first time I heard that . . .

You see, you sleep in a hammock, because you can't sleep on the ground—it rains. It rains nine months a year, continuously, there. So you build successive camps as you advance, with tree trunks, vines, palm leaves, woven to make a roof, and a hammock.

And at night—night in the forest is something truly extraordinary. All those sounds, those sounds . . . that whistling, chirring, those millions of insects and frogs all around you.

There you really begin to . . . lose yourself.

But the first night the red monkeys came, it was really fantastic!

You don't see those red monkeys. They travel generally only at night. And they travel in large groups, in the treetops. They come from very far and give out—all together—a sort of raucous howl. A howl . . . such as I've never heard in my life. It's their way, I guess, of scaring off their enemies or something like that. So you hear that formidable prehuman howling, you know, rising from out there, from the depths of the forest, and it rises and rises and rises, becoming a sort of formidable prehistoric chorus. . . . You wonder if they are not coming after you! But of course, they are not in the least interested in humans. And they pass overhead.

34

. . . That animal clamor is like a revolution. It's something extraordinarily poignant. Then the howling fades away, fades away, disappears, and silence returns.

Such an extraordinary silence after that howling wave.

And suddenly, you become aware of a little bit of self in you again . . . and you feel so . . . so much at the beginning of the earth of man—so small, tiny, fragile. What is the meaning of this little breath in the night, in the middle of the great forest? What is it?

So . . . there again, another suit of clothes falls off.

You're face to face with something very close to the roots . . . very . . . Yes, the roots of mankind: when for the first time a human being listened to THAT and said to himself: What? What is this "me," so tiny amid all this?

(short silence)

You can't put any words on it, but at that moment there's a certain way of BEING, you know, a certain VIBRATION of being that's utterly pure, utterly free of all words—just a . . . little "me" at the beginning of the world, listening.

TOWARNICKI: *That's also an intuitive experience of all the evolution one can go through, isn't it?*

It's the very question of man.

There you touch the very being of man, when all thoughts are gone, when he is rid of all his academic, social, familial jumble. When he is truly the "very first man in the world," all alone with that fantastic chorus of red monkeys, that howling wave on the move. . . . They jump from branch to branch, traveling from afar like a wave. . . . It sounds as if they were BEATING their chest, as if . . .

35

There's no room for you in that!

There's no room for you. You're a TOTAL stranger in that world. Or else you say to yourself: What? Who? Who am I in this? What is "me"?

There's just that kind of throbbing of self in you, without words, without even a question—just a "throbbing" in the midst of that huge world.

TOWARNICKI: *And it's the beginning of an answer?*

It's the beginning of something that IS. Everything else is noise, adventures, and so on. But that brief instant when you are like a pure question, a pure breath, before the hugeness of the world—that simple "throbbing of being" has an . . . unsurpassed quality.

You realize that . . . it's the very being of your being, the definition of the first man in the world, his very meaning— yet it's just a throbbing of BEING. Nothing more.

TOWARNICKI: *How long did you stay in the forest?*

I spent one year deep in the jungle. A whole year.

But there's nothing mysterious in what happened.

It was . . . marvelous, you see. There I learned . . . I learned things that I didn't know: a PHYSIOLOGICAL communion with a world into which I had thrown myself body and soul. An ACCORD with the world.

TOWARNICKI: *Did you ever come close to an accident?*

Never! I never even "thought" of the possibility of an accident! Except for the first three days when I experienced that state of cataclysm—my clothes were torn off me and I was lost. After that, it was finished! Death was unthinkable; accidents were unthinkable!

TOWARNICKI: *Did you ever consider staying there forever?*

No, not at all! In fact, this is what happened.

After ten or eleven months in the forest, I was truly very happy. I knew RUNNING moments in the forest when I felt airborne so . . . so light was I, when I was in such harmony with that world. I was . . . I had moments—more than moments; days, repeated days of true happiness.

Then—I don't remember the exact circumstances—one day I said to myself, "Goodness, you're getting to be a prisoner of this forest! You're a prisoner. . . . You're becoming a bourgeois of the forest! You're hooked!"

Suddenly, that really gave me a jolt.

Three days later I was back in my rowboat—I left everything. And I came back down to Cayenne. It was all over. I decided: "I'm going to Brazil."

I don't know what happened, but all of a sudden I said to myself, "Why, you've become a prisoner!"

I had put another suit of clothes on—the clothes of the man of the woods. I was very comfortably going round and round in it, and I could have continued for forty, fifty years, and died in the forest. And then what?

My secret still eluded me!

My secret—it's as if you could seize hold of it only when your clothes were torn off you.

Whereupon you immediately put new ones on. You immediately returned to another habit of being, to another routine, which could be quite pleasant, more or less beautiful and vast, but which was nevertheless a rut. And you found yourself the prisoner of a small happiness or a great happiness, a small adventure or a great adventure But you were a prisoner. And I didn't want to be a prisoner—of ANYTHING or ANYBODY.

TOWARNICKI: *André Breton speaks of settling down in adventure, in mystery* . . .

That's it! You settle down in the law of the outlaw.

And that's suddenly what I felt one day: "Why, I'm . . . I'm settling down in the law of the outlaw!"

Brazil: Millions for Nothing

TOWARNICKI: *So you made your decision* . . .

Oh, I didn't waste a minute! Because . . . when I decide something, it's decided. I jumped in a rowboat and returned to Cayenne. And I packed my bag: "All right, I'm going to Brazil."

I spent a week in Cayenne—rather awful, I must say—then I took a plane and landed in Belem, on the Amazon River.

There I had all sorts of new adventures.

I was rather in a dilemma in Belem. I was tempted to take a boat and go up the Amazon River. But then I thought, "You're going to repeat the experience of the jungle. You're not going to do that twice, are you?"

So I left Belem and wandered around. I took trucks and all sorts of transportation to Bahia. Once in Bahia, I thought, "And what are you going to do now?"

Finally I took another truck: "Let's go to the interior of Brazil and see what happens."

TOWARNICKI: *But what did you do for a living? Did you work?*

For a living . . . I didn't even know they spoke Portuguese in Brazil! When I arrived in Belem, I thought people spoke Spanish. That's how good my education was *(laughter)*! So I picked up a few words of Portuguese out of necessity. Actually, I learned Portuguese very quickly.

But I had to earn a living! I had to do something.

So with the last money I had in Bahia, I decided: "I'll take a truck and go to the interior, and we'll see what happens." Well, I can always work with my hands, do something.

On the way (from Bahia I went up through what is called the *Sertão*, a desert-like region in Brazil), I came down with a terrible fever.

In my truck, I just didn't know; perhaps I had contracted malaria or something. But I wasn't worried, because I totally ignored illness; I couldn't have cared less. I didn't believe in illness. But since I was burning with fever, the truck driver dropped me off in a village, laid me down somewhere, and just left me there. And off he went. I was all alone with my fever.

So that, too, was another . . . another kind of ordeal.

I didn't have a penny left. I spoke hardly three words of the local language. And I had a terrible fever whose cause I didn't know.

But it just so happened that some planters were passing by that village, and somebody told them, "There's a gringo lying over there, and he's sick." And those planters happened to be French! I don't know if you can imagine, in a tiny remote village in the middle of Brazil, some French planters happening to pass by and someone telling them, "There's a gringo dying over there. Will you do something?"

They put me in their pickup truck and took me away. . . . They had a cocoa plantation.

I recovered very well and very rapidly, because I just don't believe in illness. Certain things need to be purged, that's all.

TOWARNICKI: *A cocoa plantation—that's the land of the golden fruit!*

Yes, it's very pretty, actually. It's . . .

TOWARNICKI: *It's yellow, isn't it? Do you remember the colors?*

It has a pink color. The first cocoa leaves are pink. They're very pretty, those very first leaves. The cocoa trees are not very tall; they're more like big bushes, if you like. And covered in all shades of pink.

They grow in the *Matta*—that's what they call the forest. There are no big mountains, just small hills with hollows and streams—small running streams. It's very pretty.

And immediately one of the planters said, "Do you know how to ride a horse?" "But of course, I know how to ride a horse!" I said. Naturally, I had never sat on a horse in my life, but I had to . . . to play my role, to be capable.

They took me along on horseback.

And everything went marvelously. The horse was very gentle, and I was ready for anything. They made me go at full gallop through the *Matta*. They, too, were putting me to the test to see if I could hold my own.

Finally, a sort of friendship grew between us. Three weeks or a month after my arrival, they took me aside: "How would you like to grow cocoa with us? We'll give you a plantation."

And they took me on horseback to a very pretty place. There were a small *riachon* (it's a small stream) and a *Matta*. There were big hills, forests. . . . And one or two hills were covered with cocoa trees. They said, "It's all yours for the taking." And there was also a small, rather dilapidated house—it was away from everything.

I looked at all that . . . and I pictured myself as a "planter" . . . planter—planter for life, you know.

Suddenly I saw the whole picture: "What on earth am I doing here! So I'll grow cocoa and take my bags of cocoa and weigh them in the village. And I'll follow the market price (there is a stock market for cocoa) to make sure to sell my bag of cocoa 50 cruzeiros more than the week before, if possible."

I saw myself amid all that and I thought, "No, this is not possible!"

The next day I was gone. It was all over. I left behind some very disappointed planters. And I went down toward the south, in the *Minas Geraes*.

I had to earn a living—I had nothing.

Minas Geraes is north of Rio de Janeiro.

I became a prospector of mica. I had to make some money. There are mica mines, a lot of mica mines, in Brazil. And mica happens to be a rather rare mineral. So I started to prospect for mica for a local company, which had a small field office in one of those remote villages that you can only reach on horseback or by jeep. And by jeep, there are actually two ways to go.

Either it rains a lot or it's extremely dry. When it rains, the roads are like grease. And as soon as the sun comes back, that muddy road becomes as if "frizzled" by the heat and it feels like a corrugated sheet of metal. So there are two ways to drive on that: either very slowly or at breakneck speed.

Those are the two ways to travel: on horseback or by jeep.

So I searched for mica. . . . I was in the mica business for . . . I don't know, five or six months. The business was owned by an American, an American from Boston. An elderly American, a very nice man, actually, very, very nice and very wealthy, without children. And he liked me very much because . . . I took risks. And in whatever I did, I strove to be efficient. So if I did something, it had to be done as perfectly as possible. And I found a lot of mica.

(short silence)

So he thought of making me the heir to his business, of adopting me as his "son."

It was rather appealing.

He would call me to Rio de Janeiro, because his office was in Rio. He had a yacht. He knew I loved sailing. He said, "Here, this is your boat!" So I started to sail in Rio de Janeiro Bay. It was very beautiful. At last I was on a boat again! And, of course, I found a pretty Brazilian girl—she was beautiful. And there are a lot of lovely islands in Rio de Janeiro Bay. . . .

Rio de Janeiro: The Red Island

TOWARNICKI: *So again, here you are caught in a trap from which you must disentangle yourself. . . .*

Exactly!

The thing is, you don't immediately realize it's a trap.

But one day I realized it. I had sailed to an island in the bay—Rio de Janeiro Bay is really very beautiful. An island covered with red flowers: red flame trees. And there was an old house on it that was supposed to have been occupied by an Austrian, I think. It was truly a stunning place. The gardens were dotted with Greek Venuses; the rooms were full of antique furniture. . . . Oh, really an extraordinary place, and in the middle of nowhere. And I was with that Brazilian girl.

But one evening, I looked at it all. . . . You know, there are moments in life when your eyes open and rest there, fixed, and every detail around is suddenly engraved. You don't know why or how.

My eyes were fixed on that little beach, on that very nice and lovely Brazilian girl beside me, and the mica mines over there, and the yacht awaiting me. I said to myself, "But what are you DOING here! What on earth are you doing!"

I couldn't take one more minute of it. . . . It was just—I just couldn't. That's all. That very evening we sailed back to Rio. I went to see the charming old American and said to him, "I'm leaving." "For where?" he said. "Africa," I replied. He thought I had gone completely mad! He really thought I had gone mad.

During the few months I had prospected for mica, I had saved a little money. I went to the Compagnie Transatlantique and said, "Do you have a ship leaving for Africa? And what's its destination?" I was told that some luxury liners bound for France made a stop in Dakar. Good, I said. And I bought a steerage ticket for . . . Dakar. And I really had nothing, just enough to pay the passage to Dakar.

I don't know why, but I left everything. . . . Or rather, I know that suddenly I saw a trap. I saw myself caught in a trap. I thought, "What! You're going to end up as a fat millionaire owning mica mines? And then making little Brazilians, or Franco-Brazilians, who will make little Franco-Brazilians? . . ." I just couldn't bear it.

But why envy? People have the fate they choose. . . .
And the fate they choose is probably good for them. It's probably the best possible thing that can happen to them.
My way is not the "best" way, you know; it's just MY way.

Africa: Losing Oneself

. . . When I arrived in Dakar, I had to find a hotel room—the hotels were jam-packed, full of people. I took a taxi to look for a hotel. And I was watching the taxi meter going up and up and up, ticking away my last remaining francs. Finally I found a hotel, a hovel rather, in a suburb of Dakar. I was offered a room to share with "someone." And the first thing this "someone," a young man who was occupying the room (there were two beds, one for him, one for me), the first thing he says to me is: "I hope you don't mind sharing the same room with a Jew?" "Well . . ." I said. "Why should I? Jews are very nice people! All the Jews I have met were very generous people."

Why did he . . . I couldn't understand his question.

I was really taken aback, you know. For me a Jew, a Black, a Chinese were all human beings. I never understood how people could see a difference. That was beyond me.

And that nice fellow was so moved by my completely natural reaction that he said, "And what are you up to?" "Well," I replied, "I'm broke and I'd like to visit Africa. There's the Sahara Desert in Africa, and that's where I'd like to go. I'd really like to go to Zinder." That's what I told him.

He laughed. "Listen," he said, "my means are limited: I sell Larousse dictionaries . . . to Blacks. If you'd like, we can sell Larousse dictionaries together."

The proposal sounded rather . . . odd.

For the life of me, I couldn't picture myself selling dictionaries!

But then, why not? I had come that far.

So we started to go from village to village, from truck to
truck. . . . We traveled through Sudan, Guinea, the Ivory
Coast, Dahomey, Niger. We went up . . . all the while selling
dictionaries, which in fact sold quite well, allowing us to pay
our hotel bills and travel farther.

I arrived in Zinder, which was my obsession.

I wanted to experience the "Sahara Desert."

I wanted once more to touch an element. All my life I have
found that one can only breathe in an element, whether it's
the sea, the jungle or . . . To experience an element.

I arrived in Zinder. The rainy season had just started. I
was told, "The road is closed." So I was stuck there, right in
the middle of Africa, unable to realize my dream, which was
to plunge body and soul into the Sahara Desert and to . . .
LOSE MYSELF a little. Actually, I very much liked "losing
myself."

Losing myself . . .

TOWARNICKI: *This time, you wanted to measure yourself
with the desert?*

I wanted to plunge into it.

I wanted to plunge into it and see what would happen. Or
disappear, if necessary.

I lived each second of my life as . . . as if I were ready to
throw it out the window. For me, life had sense only if I was
able to capture that special rhythm in my body which
sometimes happened, unexpectedly, as in the jungle, the

Brazilian *Matta* or *Sertão*. . . . All of a sudden, for a few minutes, there was another kind of rhythm. And that was "IT," at last.

> **TOWARNICKI:** *You first learned this with the sea, then with the jungle.*

Yes.

> **TOWARNICKI:** *And now you were expecting an answer from the desert?*

Yes. That's where I was about to enter and . . . probably get lost because I was unable to continue. I was told, "You can't go farther; the road . . . the trail is closed. It's the rainy season. It's closed to traffic."

> **TOWARNICKI:** *So no desert?*

No desert.
I was stuck in Zinder.
But then, there was something else. . . . I still had the *Life Divine* with me. That's the only thing that followed me everywhere.

> **TOWARNICKI:** *The Life Divine by? . . .*

Sri Aurobindo. Yes, that's what I was looking for—a "divine" life. Well, I didn't know what "divine" meant, but let's say a . . . "breathable" life, a REAL life. Not a three-piece suit who is a philosopher, a mathematician or a breadwinner. . . . Not just a suit of clothes in which you go round and round, until you're put into a coffin; and then your son takes over.

I just couldn't live like that.

The "divine" life, for me, was a life where you could breathe. It was the moments when you were attuned to something . . . at once so vast and so "yourself." And yet there was no "self" in all this! It's as if . . . the whole world were throbbing in you; those moments were . . . utterly "full" and simple.

And that's what I had felt in flashes, here and there, throughout my life.

That's what I was looking for, that "divine" life.

TOWARNICKI: *The disappearance of the ego?*

You can say that, but I wasn't looking for a philosophical concept. I was looking for a particular way of breathing.

And in spite of everything, there was that "gaze," that "Sri Aurobindo" over there . . . who had looked at me in that way.

I was very, very sad when I learned he had "died," as they say. That gaze was no longer there. But the "Mother" was still there. She was with Sri Aurobindo. She was his companion.

I said to myself, "After all, there may be a secret for me there? . . ." Because I could see the picture, as it were: You add one adventure + one adventure + one adventure, but sooner or later the circle closes and you end up as a professional of the jungle, a professional of plantations, a professional of sailing. . . . You confine yourself, you see. You close yourself in, as it were. You put on another suit of clothes.

Was it conceivable that they had the . . . PERMANENT secret over there?

TOWARNICKI: *Over there, where?*

47

With Sri Aurobindo, in Pondicherry.

I thought, "How about going there and seeing for myself?"

But I was also scared, because it was an "ashram." It was more walls. But I felt, "At least, there's one person there. There's the 'Mother,' Sri Aurobindo's companion. Perhaps there is a secret awaiting me?"

So I bought a plane ticket with my remaining money, and I left . . . to go back to India . . . and try to find the secret. But not just a fleeting secret—the Thing that would be THE way of breathing each minute of the day. Something constant, something free of any clothes—something natural!

(short silence)

Nobody lives naturally.

Everything in life is artificial. Everything. The moment you become integrated in something, that thing, no matter what it is, becomes artificial.

I had to find . . . the state where you live without artifice, where something in you just THROBS, just gives out the human "sound," as it were. And therefore you experience the plenitude of what you are.

So I went back to India.

I was thirty.

And that's . . . another adventure. But a radical one. Not an adventure that comes full circle and makes you a prisoner.

That was really . . . THE Adventure. The one that does not confine you.

TOWARNICKI: *The one you are still in today?*

Oh yes! Oh yes, certainly. . . .

It's the only . . . possible way to breathe.

DAY THREE

The End of Yogis

| Second Trip to India:
| The Ashram, Mother's Gaze

TOWARNICKI: *You are now about to wander the roads.*
Nobody quite knows what's happening around you,
in you—still the same problem, in fact. So let us start
our first conversation on India, where you returned
after a trip to Egypt.

SATPREM: No, the trip to Egypt was years before, the first
time I came to India. This time, I came directly to Pondicherry.

I was actually very scared.

I was scared. . . . I knew that—I had gone through many
adventures and I thought, "Well, this one . . ." To see the
Mother (the Mother was Sri Aurobindo's companion), to go
to that ashram—I sensed one couldn't afford to bungle *that*

adventure. And if it was bungled or unsuccessful, then it would mean an endless round of dead-end adventures. Something . . . something *had* to happen.

(short silence)

But Mother . . . I had seen her with Sri Aurobindo before that whole circuit of mine. And she had . . . she had a different kind of gaze from Sri Aurobindo.

A different kind of gaze.

In fact, what had overwhelmed me when I had seen Mother was her gaze. . . . It seemed that, for the first time, someone was looking at me with love.

It was a gaze that . . . went deep into your chest and pierced something open there—a rather overwhelming experience, and a bit . . . scary, you know. I was leery of it.

But nobody had ever looked at me that way.

Nobody had shown me that love.

I had met . . . first, there was my own mother, who loved me very much. A wonderful—wonderful—woman, truly my mother, and not just in terms of passports and birth certificates.

But in all the gazes I had seen, deep down, there was always something trying to "take" or EXPECTING something of you.

But here, with Mother, it was quite strange. There was mainly a sort of "power" of love. And you felt that it didn't seek to take anything, just plunged deep, deep, deep inside you, like a . . . SWORD, as if seeking to TOUCH the roots of your being.

That gaze had very much struck me.

It was not like Sri Aurobindo's. Sri Aurobindo looked at you . . . and you felt immensity, infinity. You felt as if you were melting there, moving through centuries and centuries, and it was soft, and it was like a great snow. And you lost yourself there, and it was . . . Oh, there were no more words; it was all over, and you felt so . . . so comfortable! You felt so at home, in a country you had known forever.

But with Mother it was . . . it was quite extraordinary—it was a sword. But a sword filled with love. It wasn't something trailing into infinity; it went straight down into matter, into the "heart" (for me, at least).

It was very, very perplexing, fascinating, and . . . a real question for me. Because there was no mistaking the truth of that gaze—it went too deep. And in fact, I came back BECAUSE of that gaze. I wanted to understand. That sort of sword she drove into your innermost being—I wanted to know where exactly it went. If it went anywhere! And I was ready to go there as well. That's what interested me.

So I arrived in Pondicherry.

I was thirty.

And I really didn't feel comfortable. I dreaded that ashram.

I remember walking to the seashore. There were catamarans beached on the sand, and I hid behind one of them to smoke my cigarette. I thought to myself, "Well, my dear fellow, this is your last cigarette. You're about to join an ashram." *(laughter)* I didn't feel terribly at ease in that . . . situation. But anyway.

In the evening, I went to the ashram Playground, where all the disciples gathered. And Mother used to go there, too.

It was an ashram where they did a lot of physical exercises. And I watched while all the disciples formed into ranks and practiced an "exercise-march." I was terror-stricken. I said to myself, "I'm taking the first train out of here. I'm getting out of here! I can't take this. I can't stay here!"

But . . . I am very stubborn. I am Breton. I had told myself, "You'll try for two years. You're not going to give up at the

51

first obstacle."

So I stayed.

But I must say that I fought for YEARS—for YEARS. And only Mother could . . . keep me there. Because it was so contrary to my nature—the world of an ashram was so contrary to my whole sense of freedom, open sea, vastness. . . . Only Mother could keep me and make me understand.

Make me understand something else.

But I fought with her. Really—I can't call it anything else—I fought for . . . one, two, three years. Actually, I fought for almost six years. And I would leave the ashram. And I would come back. And leave again.

(short silence)

But one day I decided: "This time I'm leaving. I CAN'T stay here any longer. I can't take it." Can't take it because of my conditioning . . . Can you imagine Pondicherry, a small colonial town with a bandstand, sepoys, and so on? It was a whole world that was simply dreadful for me. It was so contrary to my way of breathing.

So one day I decided: "I can't stay here. I can't take it anymore. I'm leaving."

I had met a Sannyasi. And I said to myself, "I'm going to join that Sannyasi."

TOWARNICKI: *What is a Sannyasi?*

A Sannyasi is a sort of monk. "Monk" is just a word, you understand. It has nothing to do with a particular religion. They are people who have burned everything, renounced everything—who wage an all-out revolution, so to speak. That is, they renounce EVERYTHING. And they wander the roads as beggars.

52

So I thought, "Well, maybe this is the ultimate . . . adventure?" To burn everything, to go to the end—I mean, the end of the END! I had to find what was inside this human flesh.

That was it. That's what was driving me. It had nothing to do with philosophy or literature. It was a deep need of my being—a need to know who that man was in whom I went about, so clumsily, on two legs.

So I left.

I went to Ceylon to join that Sannyasi.

And thus began a very strange adventure, which was extremely enlightening for me, in a "negative" way.

Ceylon: The Temple, Divine Music

So I traveled to Ceylon, to the south of Ceylon.

He was in a temple. He lived there, as a beggar, in the temple.

I arrived there. I put on a loincloth (what is called a *dhoti*, made of white cloth), a scarf around my neck. And then . . . well, I slept in the temple, on the flagstones, because it was the only place where you could sleep. I ate whatever the Sannyasi got from begging. And I made a point to be like everybody else, so I put white ashes on my forehead. And I lived there. . . .

Life in that temple in southern Ceylon was another kind of . . . cataclysm for me, as in the jungle, as . . . All of a sudden, I was thrust into SUCH a different world, so different and yet—I can't say what I found or felt there, but I was suddenly in the midst of another kind of cataclysm.

I have no words for it.

That's it: it's always, always like clothes falling off. The clothes fall off and you find yourself completely NAKED, thrust into something totally different. Amid the gongs, the rituals; sleeping on the flagstones of the temple, begging for food. . . . I was in a completely . . . "eccentric" world, as it were, outside of any center I knew. Thrust . . . into something very strange.

I got sick almost immediately, of course, because I drank the water from the river. We begged for our rice—we were given rice full of spices (what they called *chilies*), which burned my guts. I was soon in rather bad physical shape.

But then, one of the first nights . . . You see, I was so "off center," as it were. I had no more center. And sick on top of it, at the "end" of a certain kind of life. So one night, in the temple, I had an experience—perhaps the most fantastic experience of my entire life. I heard a . . . divine music in my sleep. A music . . . I can't say. NOTHING, NO human music can approach it. It's like a "sound" that's the sound of the world—of the universe. Together with a harmony of a sublime beauty. I don't know what "divine" is, but that was "divine." Beethoven—I used to love Beethoven (the only thing in the Western world that touched me was music), but even the most sublime Beethoven quartets were like Muzak compared to that . . . BREADTH of sound, as if the whole UNIVERSE were . . . ringing, reverberating—were music.

That was an absolutely overpowering experience. When I woke up, I sat, I don't know, two or three hours with my head in my hands, repeating to myself, "This isn't possible! This isn't possible. This isn't possible. What's happening? . . ." I was like a madman from having heard that . . . that Beauty. That marvelous Beauty. I was like a madman. I kept saying to myself, "This isn't possible. This isn't possible. This isn't possible." It was such a . . . divine Beauty—it was the Divine.

I don't know what I came into contact with that night. Probably I had been so BROKEN from my usual world that I

must have come into contact with a realm . . . a realm . . .
another realm, you know.

The Sannyasi

So I followed that Sannyasi.

We traveled back up north, through Ceylon. And we returned to India.

And one day he said, "Now you are going to become a Sannyasi."

(short silence)

That morning, we were by a river. He said, "Take off your clothes."

I went into the river.

He said, "Dip yourself in."

I dipped into the river.

Then he said, "Take a little water in your hand."

I took some water in the palm of my right hand, a few drops.

He said, "Now you will perform the rituals, the last rituals, of your family: you have no father, no mother, no country; you have nothing."

I took the water and let it run through my fingers, giving it back to the river.

All the while he chanted Sanskrit mantras, which were of such great beauty. Sanskrit is a language that . . . it's like resounding bronze. And those mantras had such an old, old vibration to them. You felt as if transported thousands of years back in time.

It's as if each gesture . . . drew thousands of years in its wake. As if, suddenly, there were a depth so . . . so immense, so extensive through the sands of time. As if the gestures we were making had many, many, many lives, had been made many, many times before. Everything had such a . . . beautiful . . . depth to it. . . . It was as if . . . sacred. And I don't know why it was sacred, but . . . there were many centuries in it: in those gestures, those sounds . . . that ritual.

So I poured the drops from my hand into the river.

I was naked.

He said, "Come."

We walked to a small temple. There were other Sannyasis. We made a fire. I was naked before the fire. I sat before the fire. And the Sannyasis started to chant Sanskrit mantras.

He told me the gestures, the things I had to do. But it was always the same gesture: you "threw" into the fire (in the symbolic form of a grain of rice or oil or clarified butter). You threw . . . everything. You even threw mental realizations. You threw EVERY possible realization. You put everything into the fire. You put good, evil, sorrow, joy. All the "yeses" and "nos" of the world. You threw in everything: I don't want joy, I don't want sorrow, I don't want good, I don't want evil. I want the Thing that IS—that IS unchanging, always. THE Thing . . . that does not vary.

(short silence)

And when that holocaust was over, he gave me an orange-dyed piece of cloth (a sort of *dhoti* or loincloth, I don't know what to call it) that you wrap around yourself, a necklace of *rudraksha* beads, for reciting mantras, and a copper bowl for my water and food. And I was nothing, except that beggar who had burned everything.

Then I wandered the roads. I left. I went through all sorts of things.

He came along with me for a while. He made me take train after train after train, all across India; sleep in railway stations amid the whistle of steam engines. He was trying to . . . BREAK me in yet another way.

I spent weeks in Indian trains, in suffocating heat, filth everywhere, sleeping on railway platforms. And the mosquitoes and everything. . . . It was a kind of nightmare in which I no longer knew night from day or whether I was sleeping or walking.

It seemed . . . as if there were nothing left to break.

There was nothing left to break. I was . . . beyond and outside. . . . You couldn't break that.

TOWARNICKI: *But you were still in expectation of something?*

Yes—to know WHERE it all leads. WHERE does it all lead?

And I went up to the Himalayas.

I traveled some more.

But fairly soon, something happened . . . because . . . I was really after . . . what IS, what is TRUE, you know.

And that grace, which is always there, gives you answers.

The Naked Sannyasi: What Then?

One day, in the Himalayas, I met what is called a *Nanga-Sannyasi.*

That's a naked Sannyasi.

He doesn't even wear a loincloth; he has nothing. He's naked.

He was young, he was handsome! He was handsome; he went singing along the roads. He was naked, with just a *cimta.* (This type of Sannyasi must light a fire wherever he

57

stops; so they always carry what is called a cimta—a sort of fire tongs.) And those fire tongs clanged as he walked, you see—they resonated.

Thus he went singing along the roads, naked, with his resonating cimta. And he was so full of joy. . . .

I decided to walk along with him.

Then I said to him, "Listen, I want to get rid of these clothes."

I was . . . ASHAMED of those Sannyasi clothes! It seemed to me to be a sort of . . . disguise, a parody, to have to dress "as a Sannyasi" (in quotation marks), with clothes of a particular color!

One had to be COMPLETELY NAKED!

TOWARNICKI: *You mean, it was like a uniform?*

Yes, another kind of uniform. Another way of saying: *I* am this or that. I suddenly developed a revulsion for all that . . .

So I said to him, "I want to be naked like you."

And I looked at my white skin, which remained so dreadfully white—that stigma of the West.

I had nothing against the West! I am not being disparaging. I have nothing against it. It's just that I had that "white skin," you know, which made me look different from those people who are all tanned by the sun and . . .

Then he said, "But you can't get rid of your Sannyasi clothes! You can't; it isn't your law! You're a Sannyasi and you must . . ."

I squeezed his arm: "What law?"

"But you're a Sannyasi, . . ." he said.

I began to feel . . . stifled by that label, and I thought, "Damn! I'm in a prison again. I am a 'Sannyasi.' Hence I can't do this or that! . . ." I began to feel hemmed in again.

I asked him (in whatever language we could communicate, which was a sort of poor English), "All right, you walk the roads . . . and you walk the roads. How long are you going to walk like that? What then?"

"Well," he said, "then I walk some more!"

—"But AFTERWARDS? AFTERWARDS?"

"Well," he said, "when it's over, it's over. Your body gets burned. And it's over! You're free."

My whole being was suddenly filled with an incredible outrage.

So we WALKED through all this, SUFFERED through all this, LIVED through all this just to end up tossing it all into the fire like an old rag!

But what's the sense of this life, then?

Not to mention that I had seen all those yogis, you know, who looked so serene. I had seen them! I had sat with them! I too had meditated! I had closed my eyes. And I knew their . . . serenity! I knew how to . . . turn off a certain way of being and, well, everything becomes vast, smiling, vast—no more problems!

But what AFTERWARDS?

This was my constant question: What afterwards? What afterwards?

You remain in contemplation? You're in a state of . . . let's say "serenity" or "joy" or . . . (I can't say joy; I can't say I experienced joy). But I knew immensity—that immensity without a ripple. There's a sense of wideness; one feels so at ease there, so well. And there's a sort of great light. But when you open your eyes again . . . you find all of humanity unchanged! You find yourself unchanged, subject to hunger, cold, fear, conflicting thoughts rising from below.

And then, then WHAT?

Is the aim of life really to . . . go and sit in some remote corner of the Himalayas and remain in contemplation until the end? Is that it?

And what then?

TOWARNICKI: *Did you see any yogi performing feats?*

Of course! There is no lack of quacks. The more feats they perform, the more certainly they are quacks. Oh, yes, all their tricks are the easy part. That's just . . . showmanship. It has nothing to do with the truth.

The "truth" (I don't like that word) is something one breathes. It's like the smell of a plant, like the wind in the trees, you know. It's like a gust of wind at sea. For me, that's what the truth is. It's something that flows, that one can breathe through the pores of one's skin.

But at the end of that long course—"through the pores of one's skin" . . . there were no pores left! You simply went up and up on a sort of point of being, like the extreme point of a flame, or a candle, that rises and rises and rises, and disappears and . . . there are no more problems! A very happy state. But . . . What afterwards?

I wanted something that would fill me . . . while walking down the street or drinking scotch if necessary! While doing . . . while living life, you know! Something that would fill me every second of the day and would depend neither on a Himalaya nor on a monk's garb! I wanted something not dependent on anything.

And that's where that SWORD—that sword of light that Mother's gaze was—drew me back. Because *that* was not something that "soared upward" and left you with a feeling of vastness and serenity and . . . bliss. Quite the contrary, it was something that went DOWN into your flesh and sought to touch something there, in the depths of your being.

So that gaze brought me back to Pondicherry. I said to myself, "You've fled. You didn't have the guts to face THAT."

And so I came back to Pondicherry.

The Roads of India

TOWARNICKI: *Can we talk about those roads, the roads of India, Satprem?*

I came down the Himalayas. I took the road back to the south.

Yes, there is that great beauty of India: those people, those beings of India, and that great gentleness you meet everywhere. Everywhere you go, they open their door to you. Everywhere you go, you're welcomed with a smile. And there's something in them that understands. You don't need to explain—they feel. That, too, was a great blessing of India.

Those people among whom you don't feel—even with a white skin—you don't feel like a "foreigner." You may not go unnoticed, kids may run after you, but you don't feel like a foreigner. And they feel who you are. You don't deceive them; they feel who you are.

So, yes, there was that great gentleness of India. And then that whole dimension of . . . of the temples of India. Yes, that could have . . . caused me to lose myself definitively, more so than the Himalayas.

There was such a beautiful . . . vibration in some of those temples. You don't know Sanskrit, but . . . it's such a "full," such a "dense" language, so . . . invested with power. You just don't know where that language comes from. It gives the feeling of coming from . . . something before man. The sounds do not seem to express a language as we know it, with subjects, prepositions and direct objects. The sounds seem to . . . to have a power and to "express" something.

And those temples had that VIBRATION, which for me was extremely . . . fascinating. You felt like singing with them, dancing with them. . . . There was something extremely captivating.

TOWARNICKI: *The temple of Shiva?*

Yes, the temple of Shiva. Yes, especially the one in Benaras, which is so extraordinary. You feel you can very easily lose yourself there.

Though, I must say, I had known something similar in Egypt.

Egypt

The first time I went to Egypt, it was right after the war. I knew nothing; I was really a good little boy from the West. For me, Asia was simply geography. And I knew absolutely nothing, zero, about the religions, the spiritual traditions of the East. I was a complete layman (by layman I mean that I had read a lot of things on the subject; I was full of Western culture). But I went and spent three weeks near Luxor.

And that's where, inexplicably, I was transported into a sort of state of elation. I couldn't walk through these temples —yet they seemed completely dead, falling to pieces—I couldn't walk through them, or touch those stones, without being overwhelmed with an emotion beyond any understanding, thought or feeling. It was inexplicable. I couldn't understand. . . . But it had an incredible PHYSICAL impact on me.

You see, for us Westerners, everything is sort of clearly delimited: this is a rock, this is a chair, this is a gentleman, this is a lady. Everything is sort of confined in a precise, well-defined, limited frame. Each thing is defined.

Now that I look back at the West from . . . another perspective, I have the feeling that the whole intellectuality —the Western intellectual formation—is something extraordinarily juridical and military. Everything is rigid. Everything is in a box. And even humans, even humans are "defined."

And in that first contact with Egypt (and even more so in India), that little definition was suddenly thrust into a huge dimension that lay behind the little object I thought I had defined. All of a sudden, everything was plunged in depth after depth after depth. . . . And those depths VIBRATE. They vibrate.

And that vibration is what awoke something in me which . . . I couldn't define, for which I had no words. But things were no longer confined in a definition; they were suddenly embraced in an immensity that seemed to extend far back in time. And that immensity was not an abstraction; it felt like a "sound," a vibration.

As if those walls, for example, had retained centuries and centuries of gongs and rituals, and they kept on vibrating. Vibrating with what? With a call.

And in the midst of all that, I recognized my own call.

A call that was not from this time. A call that perhaps was from many times before. As if that cry, that need, was not born today, or even with this life, even with my childhood in Britanny. As if, suddenly, this whole life extended back, and this little call of today or this little fellow I was today was only a "projection" of something that went far, far, far into the past, and which vibrated and vibrated. Something that had called and called—and had been a call since . . . long, long ago.

TOWARNICKI: *Something that went far, far into the future?*

Maybe into the future! Maybe.

Because . . . when you were there, in that very ancient dimension, it felt like "eternity."

It isn't . . . PAST (I describe it, so it seems to be something very, very, very far back in time); it's eternal. . . . It's ETER-NAL. . . .

But it's an "eternity" without any projection into the future.

It's an eternity that IS. . . . I don't know.

Churches: Buddhism, Nihilism and Nirvana

TOWARNICKI: *A Christian could feel the same things in a cathedral or a church?*

Oh, absolutely!

Absolutely. He certainly can.

You see, EVERYTHING is actually a means, a pretext, to lead us to discover ANOTHER depth of ourselves.

But humans end up making the means into an end and a prison.

So those walls . . . Look, long ago, in Thebes, there were some people who said, "ENOUGH OF THOSE PRIESTS!" Churches everywhere, always. One is a Sannyasi, an Ashramite, a Catholic, a Marxist, a . . . We keep confining ourselves in a prison. All those things are excellent. Religion is excellent, Marxism is excellent. Everything is excellent—

provided it . . . helps you to reach THAT point where you begin to be a man. A man, that is, something that has its own vibration—which is so very old and so present, so eternal.

But whatever has helped you to approach that other dimension is made into an end. It becomes a dogma. It becomes a prison.

Or else it becomes the Guru (with a capital G). It becomes God (with a capital G).

TOWARNICKI: *And it's the beginning of death.*

Exactly! The moment you start "defining" something, it dies. It's dead.

So I have nothing against any Christianity, Hinduism or Marxism—I have nothing against anyone or anything.

But I . . . have something against—and strongly AGAINST—anything that imprisons people.

We've-got-the-truth syndrome, you know. It's in the bag once and for all, and that's it.

That's the falsehood I cannot stand.

I couldn't stand it in Thebes, I couldn't stand it in Pondicherry, I couldn't stand it in Paris, and I couldn't even stand it in the jungle.

The Truth is something that . . . "becomes." Something perpetually the same and forever in question, I could say, or in becoming. It isn't something you catch once and for all. It's something that . . . you must INCARNATE more and more.

"Incarnate"—yes, that has meaning for me.

To incarnate means to drive it into your own flesh.

And the point is, my whole search as a Sannyasi ended up in something that drove me *out* of my own flesh.

That's where I was at the end of that whole search—at the end of what seemed to be the ULTIMATE search. Well, for me the ultimate wasn't ultimate. Or if that was ultimate, then I sympathize with the Buddhists, with the Illusionists, with those who throw bombs everywhere, for it's the active or negative way to reach the same end.

All those practices are nothing but a damn illusion.

We are offered the choice between getting out of it all and blowing everything up.

On the one hand, yogis, Buddhists tell you, "The solution is Nirvana—go above"; and on the other hand, others tell you, "No, let's just bomb this whole damn world out of existence. . . ."

It's exactly the same thing.

One blissfully, the other diabolically, they are one and the same thing.

Two negations amounting to the same thing. Both roads are . . . dead ends.

Or else this Earth has no sense.

This was the question bringing me back to Pondicherry, to . . . Her.

Her.

TOWARNICKI: *Satprem, what is it like to walk the roads of India?*

Ah, walking is something I've always enjoyed, whatever the circumstances.

I like that sense of exhaustion when the body reaches the extreme limit of its resources. Then you start to . . . get into another rhythm. It's no longer the body exerting an effort—there's something else carrying you.

You walk and walk, and . . . you merge with a great rhythm. When you go beyond the state of fatigue, beyond a certain stage, there's a great rite that takes over.

So on the roads of India, well . . . I can't say it was MORE than anywhere else, because it was a "march," except that the people were . . . I felt I was in a country where I could breathe easier. That is truly India's grace (or was, because I don't know . . . if one could say the same thing now); it's the grace of that country. There's truly a different air.

But I had reached the end of the human question, you see, after traveling all over India, and coming into contact with or touching what its ideal was.

I had reached the end of the human.

I did not have an answer.

Or else the answer was to get out, to throw the old rag into the fire.

I did not have the answer.

And this is actually the cause of India's decay and degradation: instead of using her spirituality to INCARNATE it, she used it for dreaming, for meditation, for a kind of spiritual somnolence they call "Nirvana," but . . . these people are DOZING! They are pleasantly and vastly dozing— look, what ARE they and what are they DOING for the earth?

That's what I kept bumping against. I kept coming back to that same point and bumping against it.

What was the goal? What was the goal of this human BODY, the same body of a child on a seashore who stared at the immensity and had the feeling that there was something to be lived!

So the end of it all was closing the eyes and—and then what?

Was that the end?

But the child that I was, staring at the waves, wouldn't have accepted that for one minute!

That's not what life was! That's not what a divine life was.

And yet . . . at the very beginning of India's history, others had understood—the rishis, five or six or seven thousand years ago. They had understood something of the secret.

The same secret Sri Aurobindo and Mother discovered.

And that's what was really drawing me back. At the conclusion of that Indian tour, I was coming BACK to . . . that source—which is India's true source. And the true reason for this life.

TOWARNICKI: *It isn't in the beyond that things are to be done but here?*

If it were beyond, why on the earth would we take a body?

Like that Nanga-Sannyasi who says, "All right, it's over! I throw the old rag into the fire and . . . that's it. I am free!"

But it's . . . what is the evolutionary meaning of such a thing?

We have been flagellates, we have been frogs, we have been fish, we have been monkeys to end up . . . We have TOILED, really, for millions of years, and suffered and . . . Why? Just to end up in a little spiritual meditation?

That's intolerable!

It doesn't make any sense.

All this . . . damn story, and painful and fantastic story, climaxes in a little . . . in such a poor little thing?

If the first embryo of being began to wiggle on the earth, it must have a meaning for the earth! Truth is something that must have a meaning in this body!

Evolution does not take place in the convolutions of the brain!

It takes place in the fins of a fish. It takes place in claws. All right, for a time, it takes place in a number of convolutions that have been unduly inflated, but it isn't . . . THE WAY to the fulfillment of those millions of years.

That's not possible!

It must take place in the flesh. It must be something in the body.

And that's where Mother got me. That's how she caught me.

TOWARNICKI: *But I don't suppose you question the teaching of Buddha himself, the path leading to the unveiling of illusion and to a center of consciousness?*

Look, there's an illusory human way of living life. It's very clear. An illusion that is temporary, useful. It is obvious that there's an appearance of things that has to be broken through.

The question is to get out of the notion of . . . little objects confined in a box—we've got to get out of that box. There's no doubt about that. That's what illusion and falsehood are.

The point is to break through all at once into a truly vaster dimension.

And that's the FIRST step. It isn't the end. It's just the ABC's!

So once you've broken through that crust—that little "box" where you've confined all things and all beings—once you've pierced that . . . piece of cardboard (it's nothing but a piece of cardboard), once you've gone through that, what are you going to do with this body? What happens then?

This is the answer that none of the yogis have, none of the Illusionists have, and none of the Buddhists have.

TOWARNICKI: *Unless these are just the by-products of Buddhism?*

By-products?

TOWARNICKI: *Of Buddhism.*

But I . . .

TOWARNICKI: *Because, undoubtedly, if you go back to the origin, if you read the words of Buddha himself and the teaching of the principal Masters, that's really another level of things?*

Yes. True, there's a whole world between what the prophets or enlightened people (call them what you like) have said, and what their followers and disciples and . . . churches have made of them.

What do we know of the real words of Christ? What do we know of the real words of Buddha? We know nothing really. So when I speak of Buddhism, I am not really questioning Buddha himself so much as . . . the church that has been built around him.

TOWARNICKI: *Do you recall Sri Aurobindo's position with regard to . . . not Buddhism, but the teaching of Buddha himself?*

It's very difficult to talk about it, because Buddhism has become synonymous with a particular way of being and living. So we can only discuss it in terms of Buddhism, not in terms of Buddha. That isn't possible.

And it has been very useful. Buddhism has been very useful in the evolution of human consciousness to help us or force us to PUNCTURE certain appearances.

But it's the FIRST step!

And what's the second step?

That's it. That was my question. . . . That's where I was at the end of my journey. And I hadn't arrived there philosophically! I had arrived there as concretely as can be, because I was still that same . . . KID, in fact, staring at the immensity of the sea and . . . saying to himself, "But where is my secret? Where is THE secret of my being, of . . . this body I'm in?"

Gurus

TOWARNICKI: *But Sri Aurobindo's teaching was already enlightening you?*

Yes. But I read Sri Aurobindo . . . True, I had read some Sri Aurobindo. But, I don't know, it's as if I were reading through the pages.

As I told you, I wandered around the world with *The Life Divine.* But . . . I really wandered with the "world" of Sri Aurobindo, with his atmosphere, with what he represented. And whenever I read a page or two, it wasn't even the words I was looking at: I felt a sort of look or depth in the background, and I liked being in the company of . . . "that."

So it wasn't even his philosophy—which I knew very little of—that really attracted me.

I had finished with the intellect at nineteen. I had read hundreds and hundreds of books, and understood once and for all that no answers could be found in books.

TOWARNICKI: *So the last snapshot of that Indian tour is you as a white-skinned Sannyasi wandering under the gaze of a friendly Indian populace?*

Oh yes! They're more than friendly; they're gentle. And a true gentleness. A gentleness that isn't just a smiling face but comes from the heart. That's truly the grace of this country.

There was that great gentleness.

But I wasn't about to spend my life in a monk's skin, you see. I needed another meaning to life. I needed to touch something TRUER than all that.

TOWARNICKI: *What regions of India did you visit?*

Bengal, primarily. And I . . . well, I traveled all over India. I went up through Benaras, Brindavan, into the Himalayas. Not much in western India. But mostly the east and northeast.

TOWARNICKI: *For several months?*

It was very short. Very concentrated. Because I was really led immediately to my question. I wasn't meant to waste a single minute in my life: the moment one phase was over, I was rather brutally put before the answer I needed to hear or to LIVE.

TOWARNICKI: *Did you meet a guru or a Sannyasi who struck you?*

Oh, I met . . . lots of them.

TOWARNICKI: *Do you remember any particular story in the course of that. . . ?*

Gurus, well . . . Personally, I find gurus dreadful. I can't put it any other way. And yet . . . this is obviously a manner of speaking.

Because, in fact, EVERYTHING is the Guru.

Each instant, each thing, each encounter, each accident, each happening IS the Guru. Everything comes to show you the way. We just don't realize it. We take things in the usual way, as we have always taken them. But if we knew how to look at things, each thing IS the Guru. I mean, each thing comes to teach you, to show you the way. Each encounter, each person, each accident, each incident—this is the Guru. And so why should that be put into a particular skin . . . a skin dressed in white linen and . . . sitting cross-legged?

I can't stand—I just can't stand all those people. I see through them very quickly. I admit, some of them are absolutely sincere. But look at what their disciples make of them! That's what is repugnant.

They make them into divinities. And then it's quite convenient, you see, a guru: "Well, my guru will do that for me." It COMPLETELY relieves you from making any personal effort or going through the process yourself.

Ah! "My guru is there; he'll do it for me." The-guru-the-guru-the-guru. It's always the same old thing: the god relieves you from being . . . from becoming what you are.

Mother said it very well. She said: "It's LAZINESS . . . it's LAZINESS that makes one worship. What one has to do is become."

But to become takes guts. There's no room for dozing off, you see.

And that's what Mother's sword was all about. There you couldn't doze off. You CAN'T doze off. You can't leave it to somebody else to do it for you.

And that's why I came back.

At the end of that journey, I came back to that ashram.

I now understood that I had to overcome all my . . . phobias about walls, structures, systems—for HER, that is. I couldn't have cared less about the ashram.

But SHE was there.

SHE is the one I wanted to see.

And that's where another grace was given to me. But I think we all have the grace commensurate with our call. All depends on what we call!

And she probably felt that call in me.

And with her . . . smile, her irony, her challenge—there was always a challenge deep down in Mother's eyes. She always seemed to challenge you: "Let's see if you can. Try!"

There was really a "challenge" (I like the English word for it).

There was a challenge deep down in those eyes.

The Rock from the Ganges

TOWARNICKI: *During that tour on India's roads, did anything special happen to you? Did you see any particular sign? Were you struck by a particular incident? An event that taught you something? An animal, a surprise, a human being, an accident, something?*

I don't know. Yes . . . something struck me.

In the course of all my travels, I went to the Ganges, toward the source of the Ganges—not right at the source, but high enough up the Ganges, high up the Ganges. And as always in my life, I loved rocks. I like stones. I like rocks. For me rocks have a life of their own.

And I had picked up a rock in the Ganges that I found quite beautiful. I had kept that rock with me. And on my return journey, one day I was given shelter near a railway station. A nice man who was—I don't know, something to do with railways, maybe a ticket collector or something; at any rate, he had a little job with the railways. He lived next to the tracks with his wife, two or three children, and his old mother was also there. And they gave me shelter.

And, I don't know why, I pulled out my rock.

And the old mother kept looking at that rock. She kept looking at it; I don't know why.

Spontaneously I took the rock and gave it to her. And I said to her, "I got it in the Ganges."

Whereupon that . . . old woman put the rock before her on the floor and placed her forehead on it. It was so simple, so moving to see the . . . love with which that woman put her forehead on that rock from the Ganges.

I don't know, that touched me very much.

That CAPACITY FOR ADORATION, you know. The . . . ease or spontaneity with which they can adore. In other words, yes, merge with something wider than the little surface person, or the little object, or . . .

That deeply touched me.

I had recognized . . . something.

The Descent into the Body

Return to Pondicherry: The Body Is the Bridge

TOWARNICKI: *Are there some words of Mother's* . . .

SATPREM: Yes, certainly.

TOWARNICKI: . . . *that would give the reader the same "jolt"* . . .

Yes. Yes, certainly.

TOWARNICKI: . . . *as the person who has just arrived and doesn't yet know what "the supramental" is? Who doesn't know what going down into matter means? Who just perceives signs, inklings. So, Satprem—*

Yes.

TOWARNICKI: —*you arrive in Pondicherry.*

Yes, actually, there is a key sentence by Sri Aurobindo—there is also one by Mother—that followed me for a long time. From the moment Sri Aurobindo looked at me, in fact. And I traveled the world with that sentence, without quite understanding its implications or what to do about it.

I remember, in *The Life Divine*, he said (I am not quoting exactly): "Man is not the summit of evolution; he is a transitional being. If he does not want to surpass himself, he will be surpassed."

That sentence followed me everywhere. As if, there, he really had touched the heart of the question.

I had gone through that whole fantastic course, you know, so eventful, for so many years across the world, through so many adventures, and here I was in my Himalayas, really facing quite a . . . frightening question. For I had reached the end of all possibilities of research.

In terms of this humanity, I was before . . . two possible summits.

The summit I had perceived, and even "touched," that of the yogi, let's say. The path that rises like a sharp point toward the summit of consciousness, breaking through the sort of skull cap that confines us—and you emerge on a sort of apex of being, an extremity of being . . . in something that's obviously very fulfilling. There, all problems are gone. It's . . . timeless. It's eternal. It's like a great white silence behind everything, in the depths of everything. It fills you; it's good.

And in fact (now I understand it; I understood later), this is what I experienced, as a Breton child, when I was in my little cockleshell on the sea; and I felt so good on my boat, with the impression of melting in the breeze, the wind, the smell of seaweed—that was that same very full state.

But—and this is where the difference lies—I felt that in my body, in my nostrils, in my hands that held the helm and obeyed the current, which followed the movement of the wind and the sails.

Whereas that other thing in the Himalayas (and else-where, too) occurred after everything had sort of dissolved, after everything had fallen silent, when everything was gathered together like a sharp ascending point. Then I felt it.

But what THEN?

You open your eyes and life returns as usual, you see.

I was truly before that summit of humanity, so to speak.

Or else, there was the other summit, the summit of elec-tronics, of the Western magician who produces more and more efficient monsters—and is eaten alive by his own system.

Those were the two extremes before me: the summit of the yogi and the summit of the electronics man or the intellect.

Which one to choose?

One doesn't quite know where to sink, but one does seem to sink in both cases, either in a luminous whiteness or else in a fairly suffocating blackness.

Meanwhile life . . . divine life still eludes us!

And that's where Sri Aurobindo's sentence kept following me.

That's where it kept following me.

So I came down from my Himalayas, at a gallop this time, and . . . I returned to her. Her.

Because some of her words, too, had very much struck me.

Okay, it's all very well; you say: "Man is not the summit of evolution. We are on our way to another stage of evolution."

But how? By what MEANS?

And that's where one of Mother's sentences had very much struck me. In fact, it was the key for me.

One day, she said: "This physical body is capable of a progressive development in evolution. Through each individual formation (in other words, what we have undergone through evolution), the physical substance progresses. . . ." And she added: "And one day, it will be capable of making a BRIDGE between physical life as we know it and the life we might call supramental, as Sri Aurobindo did, the life of the next species—it's the PHYSICAL body that will make the BRIDGE."

It isn't on the summits of consciousness above, on a razor-sharp point—so sharp it ends up dissolving, vanishing—that one actually moves to something else.

Or else one moves out of humanity, out of evolution—out of everything!

It's IN THE BODY.

And that touched a deep chord in me, because I am very interested in the body. That's where I live, you see. And it's where I've always wanted to live. In all my adventures or actions (I don't know what to call it), my body together with my whole being had to participate. Otherwise, what's the point?

That's a taste I picked up once and for all while running on the moors, with the smell of furze, seaweed and spray. That had a REAL meaning for me. And the cries of sea gulls. . . . That was FULL, as it were. For me, that was already a sort of divine life.

But, of course, that kind of life is only possible for a few rare minutes at a time in an existence that . . . was not in the least divine.

So how to find, to "incarnate" that divine life?

And that was after trying or SEEING what the famous realization of yogis is—because I touched it. . . . What a fuss they make over it! They make a big fuss over nothing.

(short silence)

All right, it may be useful for a humanity sunk in matter. It's very good to step back a little, to pierce through all those layers of conditioning and emerge into a little bit of silence and all that. . . . That part is good; it's nothing to reject or sneer at. But it's like, you know, getting two minutes or ten minutes of oxygen in a 24-hour day. It's hardly a solution! Or if it's the solution, then evolution is something absurd whose culmination is withdrawal from evolution!

I am using abstract words, but actually, for me, all that had a very physical and concrete sense. Because I had touched it. I had touched that light, that vastness. And that is why I was suddenly confronted with a very pressing and agonizing question, which propelled me back from my Himalayas to . . . to Her who had said: "It's in the body. The physical body is the BRIDGE."

And this despite . . . everything that made me cringe—those walls, that ashram, all that conditioning which seemed to me as pointless in the East as it is in the West. Anything that smacks of "walls" or "school" . . . is simply unbearable for me; it suffocates me. I feel suffocated.

But, well, "She" was there, in that ashram. So I said to myself, "I must. . . . I went through the jungle. Why couldn't I go through an ashram?" Since that's how it is.

Actually, there was a grace awaiting me, because in fact there's always a grace. When you search, when you call, there's ALWAYS a hand helping you. And looking back, you realize how marvelous it was: there's such a caring, sweet, kind hand that watches over and . . . reaches out when you no longer know or can do anything on your own. Especially when you no longer can do anything yourself. That's when the grace comes.

TOWARNICKI: *What was the ashram like?*

The ashram? There were already a lot of people at the time. Perhaps a thousand people, a thousand disciples. They were, of course, scattered throughout the town, but they used to gather in a sort of central building. There were also a lot of sports activities, which is not customary in most ashrams. All the disciples were dressed in white. They looked very . . . yes, fairly at peace with themselves and not dark, apparently. Each one had certain activities, meaning there were various "services" where each disciple was supposed to work a little. And then they would come together for meditation. But the focus (at least officially, I could say), the focus was mainly on work, material activities, sports. So there was a great number of games. There was hathayoga as well as soccer, tennis and judo. There was every possible activity.

TOWARNICKI: *Sri Aurobindo was already dead then.*

Dead . . .

TOWARNICKI: *Who was Sri Aurobindo? Who was Mother? What was their relationship?*

But that's the very sense of it all!

An ashram per se does not mean anything, you see.

A being, whoever he may be, has an experience—INCAR-NATES an experience. Then the quality of that experience spontaneously "attracts" a number of people who . . . who seek to participate in the experience, or to understand what it's about.

That isn't anything new. The Greeks knew it very well. The Peripatetics, I believe, had disciples and communicated and exchanged their experiences while walking and strolling.

That's what the origin of an ashram is: A being has an experience or a certain type of realization, and disciples, as they are called, come and gather around him. Yes, but the trouble is, the number of disciples starts to grow, and the ashram—what had become an ashram through an accumulation of circumstances—well, becomes their property, and the Master becomes their property, and they are the ones who control the genuine teaching of the Master. This has been the ever-recurring story in the past, everywhere. It's the one that we . . . that I was about to witness, in fact.

TOWARNICKI: *I need, if possible, a small historical reference as to Sri Aurobindo's role in the ashram. As well as Mother's. The relationship Sri Aurobindo and Mother might have had in the past.*

All right. The action of the one who is called the Guru (for lack of a better word) or the Master—the one who has the experience—does not take place (at least, not always) through words.

Sri Aurobindo tried to explain a little what he was doing, or seeking, in his writing. For quite a long time, Mother communicated it through spoken words: there were the *Questions and Answers* in the evening on the ashram playground.

But, actually, this was not the main thing.

The main thing is the power of diffusion of the experience. It's something the West has trouble understanding because everything has to be mental. They create philosophies, you see, couched in paragraphs—it's just ideas. Whereas, here, there are no ideas; there are forces. We keep forgetting that the mind is just a dried-up little outgrowth striving to translate a living force behind.

Well, the living force is there. That's what you must come into contact with. The real work of a disciple is actually to establish a contact with the force or power of experience that is there. For it isn't something confined to a particular body. It radiates, you see, like the fragrance of a flower or a radioactive material. You have to come into contact with it and let it—that power of experience—work within you and within your own flesh. That's what a disciple should strive to do.

TOWARNICKI: *But who founded the ashram of Pondicherry?*

Well, you can't say it was "founded," that Sri Aurobindo decided to "found" the ashram at some point. That's not how things work.

It just so happened that, as I told you, disciples came like bees, all around, and it made an ashram! And one day it was decided that there was an ashram because of all those people who were there.

TOWARNICKI: *And Mother?*

This is actually what the life of an ashram is: there's the Master, and a number of bees come around him to . . . gather honey. And normally, when the Master goes, everything stops. Or else, if it continues after the master, it's just a . . . a church.

You see, the moment the core of living experience is gone, you just live on theorems; you try to apply the Master's ideas as best as you can. In short, it starts to become . . . it's the embryo of a church, or a school. And that's exactly what happened.

TOWARNICKI: *So here you are, Satprem, coming back to the ashram. How does Mother appear to you? And who is Mother?*

Mother . . . Yes, she's first of all that gaze. Very different from Sri Aurobindo's, and yet it would increasingly resemble Sri Aurobindo's. But very different.

That gaze was a sort of . . . yes, a "sword"—a sword of light. Something penetrating deep into your being and seeking to touch a root there, and you felt . . . you felt that she pierced through your being's layers or coverings to try to . . . reach something in the depths.

Mother was a power at work. That's what she was—a power. What is called *Shakti* in India.

The Impasse of Occultism

TOWARNICKI: *Who was she? Where did she come from?*

Oh, Mother's story is a long story! *(laughter)*

To start with, she was French. She was born in Paris, of a Turkish father and an Egyptian mother.

Mother's story is like a novel—in fact, Mother is the greatest adventure story I've ever known.

You can't tell all of Mother's story!

TOWARNICKI: *Yet, it must be told, a little. It must.*

(laughter) All right, then. She, too, in a way, had knocked on all sorts of doors in order to find an answer to man's condition.

Obviously, she was born with the sense that man—this human being—was not the final product, that something else had to come out of this being which would be the next "step" in evolution. She was born conscious of that.

And she knocked on many doors. She played with all Western philosophies. She played with all Western aesthetics. She was a friend of Rodin, of Monet, of . . . (who else?) of Sisley, of the great Impressionists. She tried the door of music—she was a great musician. She knocked on many doors. She was also gifted in mathematics.

And then she knocked on a very interesting, and very dangerous, door—the door of occult powers. Because, if there was to be another being, a step beyond the human, HOW was it going to . . . come into being? A rather natural answer is to say: maybe there are occult powers in man that will give the solution and open the door to another state?

Obviously, few people are capable of having this type of experience. And above all—above all—once they've tasted it, EXTREMELY FEW people are capable of getting out of it. Because it's . . .

TOWARNICKI: *This was the period of Steiner, the period of Schuré . . .*

Yes, it was the period of Schuré. It was still the period of Gurdjieff.

And Mother met someone who was called Théon. Someone who was a super-Gurdjieff—Gurdjieff was a little boy compared to Théon. A man who had a lot of occult knowledge.

We only know the laws of matter, you see. There are other laws behind, that's quite obvious. Other laws that are very powerful and very effective. And it's a blessing that humans know nothing about them because they would use them in the most dreadful ways.

But at any rate, Mother also experimented with that to see if those so-called occult methods could in fact be of use. But she realized, in several concrete examples, as Sri Aurobindo also did, that it's a bit like pulling on a rubber band: as long as you keep pulling on the rubber band, it remains taut, you see, and it can perform miracles (what we humans call miracles), but the minute you let go—poof, it's finished! Everything returns to the way it was.

There is the story of a disciple or friend of Sri Aurobindo's who had been bitten by a rabid dog. Using his occult knowledge, he stopped the progress of the disease, which was thus kept under control. It was kept under control for ten or fifteen years, I don't remember exactly. But one day, this man, who was a politician-yogi, lost his temper—he lost his self-control. Twenty-four hours later he was dead of rabies. In other words, for ten years he had kept the . . . rubber band of his consciousness taut, so to speak, and the disease was contained, kept under control—it looked miraculous to everybody but him. But let go of the rubber band, and it's over! Everything returns as it was before. These are . . . short-lived miracles. The man in the street is dazzled by it, because it can be used to do many things. It can appear quite dazzling and miraculous, but . . . it doesn't have any lasting power. It doesn't have the power of the thing that "comes from" matter directly, you see. It's something being IM-POSED on matter.

So you can indeed impose that power, that force or will on somebody's head, cure him, do this and that, but he will catch his disease again three minutes or fifteen days later. And then, in the end, we all catch death.

And if this weren't enough, there is the much greater danger of using these powers for the wrong ends. What would people immediately do with these powers? They would use them to get rid of everything that stands in their way! Or, worse, they would use them to eliminate everything that seems evil in this world.

But what do they really know about that evil?

What do they know?

Isn't that "evil," in fact, necessary to lead to something beyond it?

Humans beings know nothing.

A great vision is necessary in order to handle power.

TOWARNICKI: *But what happened after she experimented with those occult powers?*

Well, she saw that it was in fact a dead end. It was NOT the solution.

TOWARNICKI: *So what happened then?*

Well, as always, that grace is there. When you have completed an experience and there is a real call in you to go farther. . . .

She then came into contact with a philosopher who had to make a political campaign in India to run for the French

Parliament. And that is how Mother, after meeting that philosopher, was led to Sri Aurobindo.

After traveling all that course (I am skipping many details), every avenue closed one after another before her.

She clearly saw that playing with philosophies didn't lead anywhere beyond a play. Aesthetics had its limits. Music had its limits. All the great occult powers had their limits. None of that was the key to move on to . . . to a humanity that might be really human—what it scarcely is at present, or not yet.

And that is how she came to Sri Aurobindo.

TOWARNICKI: *In the ashram in Pondicherry?*

It wasn't formed when she came. There were just a few disciples. A dozen disciples or so, who didn't understand much about what was going on, but who were there. And that number of disciples grew, and became what is known as an ashram.

But the ashram is nothing! What matters is the person who IS at the center and HAS the experience, and the KIND of experience he has.

And personally, what I saw at the end of that whole journey is somebody telling me, "It's the BODY that will make the BRIDGE."

It is not occult powers. Not yogic powers. Not philosophy. Not all the knowledge of the Upanishads. None of that. It's neither the best nor the worst.

It isn't the Upanishads. It isn't even the Bhagavad Gita. Not any text. It's none of all that!

It's something else—it's the BODY.

The body doesn't have any philosophy, you see. It sleeps well, it doesn't sleep well; it's hungry, it's cold—that's what the body is.

So she was telling the secret.

And that's why I came back, to see what that "secret in the body" was.

Mother's Exploration: The Descent into the body, the Other Side of the Fishbowl

TOWARNICKI: *You now find yourself in Mother's presence.*

In Mother's presence?

TOWARNICKI: *Or whatever you like to call it. What is beginning to dawn on you through what she says. But, as she says, it's a mystery beyond any formulation. But then, how is that teaching practiced? What is the. . . ?*

But what was marvelous to me was that Mother was never a teaching!

Mother explored. She had nothing at all to teach.

For some time, she made the effort of telling the disciples, "Not this way—that way. You must . . . do this and you must do that." But once that was over, Mother was the explorer of the new species.

So she didn't know!

Mother didn't know the way!

And what is really incredible—and that's what captured my life—is that, by some mysterious grace, she made me the witness or confidant of her exploration. That is, she confided to me all her doubts, her questions, the appearances of failure—everything.

She began to speak to me the way one speaks to a child, you know, as if telling him a story. I would ask her any question that came to my mind. She answered all my questions. And slowly, slowly she led me into her own exploration. As if she wanted to make me, a human child, participate in the process of what will come AFTER the human—how one goes BEYOND the human.

But she didn't know the way.

She began that yoga in the body at the age of eighty.

And perhaps she began out of love, because the one she loved, Sri Aurobindo, was gone. He was "dead," as they say.

So Death was the enemy.

It seemed that death was the one that in the end always swallowed up Love—the one that always had the last word.

So it's as though she wanted to WREST Sri Aurobindo from death, in a way, or tear off that mask of death to see what is behind it. It's a bit like the story of Orpheus and Eurydice.

What is there behind it?

Why death?

So she took me along in that exploration, under one pretext or another. At the beginning she used to call for me, and she sat in that high-backed chair. And I sat on the carpet, listening to her. She truly knew so many things. It was wonderful to listen to her. But most importantly, little by little she started telling me about her own experience.

So what is that yoga "in the body"?

We usually think that the body is the simplest thing in the world; it's our body. It's . . . something familiar.

But how is this supposedly familiar thing going to produce something other than a replica of the same substance?

Biologists say, "It's simple. Changing the order in the molecule of DNA can produce variations." But, if anything, we all know that those variations are likely to be monstrous.

"If some cosmic ray strikes and changes the sequence of a molecule of amino acid, there can be a variation." But all this takes place over thousands and thousands of years.

So where is the solution if biology seems to say that we will never produce anything other than a human being?

Perhaps just a superhuman being in the intellectual sense. Or else a physiological monster.

But how could another species be possible?

Biology does not have an answer. It says, "Combining certain molecules may, after thousands and thousands of years, result in a variation, which will result in other variations, which will eventually create a new species."

All right, it was . . . at the time, it was 1960. It was already quite clear, then, that the world could not afford to wait thousands of years. The problem was right around the corner. An answer had to be found.

And where, in the "body," was the answer, since biologists are unable to provide it?[1]

What, in fact, is the "body"?

It seems utterly simple, but it is actually the thing we know the least. It's the one thing we know nothing about.

---

1. To tell the truth, as recently as Sept. 1988, biology stumbled upon a surprising new "fact." "In a provocative challenge to accepted evolutionary theory," reports *The Boston Globe*, "two groups of scientists are asserting that simple organisms can reengineer their own genes in response to environmental stress. New experiments show that even single-celled organisms can profit from experience and *'choose which mutations they should produce,'* say Harvard School of Public Health researchers. . . ." "It seems that bacteria are doing something one would have thought impossible," acknowledges Dr. John Cairns, the leader of the Harvard group. "My guess is that if cells have evolved mechanisms that allow them to do this, it is going to be so advantageous that it seems unlikely that higher organisms will have given that up [in the evolutionary process]. But that's sheer speculation, not science."

What do we know about our body? We are wrapped in an
. . . accumulation of successive layers. And we live mainly
in the upper layer, the mental, intellectual layer. Actually,
our entire life takes place in the mind. We never touch the
body directly—we touch it THROUGH all sorts of ideas and
habits. But what do we really know of the body itself, AS IT
IS?

Hence if we want to start discovering that body "as it is,"
biology "as it is"—not through a microscope, but as it lives—
we must begin, obviously, by piercing through that mental
"layer." That first layer, expressed by the whole racket of
our ideas, prejudices, everything we constantly live in, including all the medical suggestions, every . . . conceivable
suggestion—the whole life in which we are confined.

That is the FIRST layer to break through in order to get
closer to the body. We must first begin by silencing all that
mental racket that envelops the body.

Then, if you continue that "descent"—the "path of descent," as she called it—you encounter a SECOND layer,
which is the emotional layer. It's all the feelings we have,
all the emotional reactions we have. It's a whole teeming
world, and quite a bit stickier than the intellectual layer.
But that, too, constantly conditions our existence. And it
covers up the body. It's like a web covering the body. How
can we see anything of the cellular milieu, so to speak, as
long as it is obscured and covered over by all those layers?
We have to get through those layers.

And so, that second web, that second layer of emotions and
feelings has to be broken through in order to reach the body.

And the descent gets more and more difficult. That is, we
have to silence, or break through, all that emotional din in
us, all those reactions we are hardly aware of because they
come to us so naturally.

Then we encounter a THIRD layer. It's the layer of all the "sensations." We are getting quite close to the body. All the sensations of the body, its spontaneous reactions: fear, anxiety, aggression. . . . We discover a whole swarming world, which has NOTHING to do with the body itself. It's just the HABITS that have been cultivated in the body—habits cultivated by education or developed through atavism, habits coming from our environment. We think we CAN'T do this or that; it's impossible. We CAN'T eat this or that; we CAN'T live above a certain temperature; we CAN'T . . . The body is conditioned by a kind of enormous layer of "you can't, you can't, you mustn't," "this isn't possible, that isn't possible, that's possible." We live in a formidable conditioning.

At that point, we begin approaching something that . . . that's very (how shall I put it?) intense, acute, dangerous.

We begin approaching the roots of . . . of death in the body.

We realize that if we want to interfere with those microscopic habits covering our cellular substance—our body—if we start interfering with that, well, it causes a revolt in the body, a panic in the body, a fear.

And finally we reach bottom: a wish, a CALL for death. As if deep down in the consciousness (almost touching the body; I am not saying *in* the body, for we aren't yet in the body itself) there were something YEARNING for death—something for which life is a kind of catastrophe. Because it means constantly struggling, exerting oneself, taking, rejecting—life is a sort of constant threat.

Thus, deep in the body, we encounter a sort of yearning for rest, for inertia. As if all the old evolutionary memories were accumulated there, along with a kind of deep nostalgia for the mineral. The peace of the mineral, you know, before life was born, when everything was still static.

There is that need.

94

Deep in the body is that need for rest, for inertia—and above all for the cessation of this constant nightmare of . . . struggling, acting, reacting. All those cells are under tremendous tension, forcing them to struggle. So underneath is a yearning for death.

Mind you, this exploration is not experienced abstractly.

It is experienced through . . . through many illnesses (I am speaking of Mother, of Mother's exploration). The minute you try to interfere with the usual way of things, everything goes awry. The slightest disruption, and you see all sorts of fear and anxiety rising within the body, from everywhere: "Oh, this is death," "Oh, this is cancer," "Oh, this is such and such disease." A world TEEMING with suggestions, deep down in the body.

So you must break through all that. You must break through that illusion of disease. We must break through . . . death.

(short silence)

But the curious thing is (it's obviously difficult to summarize such a process), it's as though you were always confronted with destruction in order to find the key, the Force greater than the force of destruction—the law of destruction that . . . SEEMS to reside in the body's depths.

As you go down through the network of all those successive webs covering the body, once in a while strange infusions or permeations occur in the body, and suddenly, for a few seconds, the body finds itself in a . . . world where every law seems to have crumbled, to be inoperative! A world where all those implacable things are suddenly dissolved in something stronger than the law of death, stronger than the law of illness, stronger than—something for which all that is an ILLUSION.

For instance, Mother had countless heart attacks. Well, normally you die from that. But just when she was on the verge of death, as it were, something else intervened, like a few seconds of . . . light or power that suddenly, pfft, blew that apparent accident out of existence. And the illness was gone! The heart attack was gone. It no longer had any reality.

But then, the experience has to recur once, twice, a hundred times for the cells of the body to begin to get accustomed to this "other law" where all the old suggestions dissolve.

The body can only "learn" slowly another possibility.

But what is fantastic (when we have the guts to go through all those layers) is that we suddenly realize that all those inexorable "laws" confining us—the laws codified by medical science, mathematics, physics—are all an immense . . . illusion. They have no reality! At a certain depth or cellular PURITY (once we have reached the origin of cellular life free of all its coatings and coverings), at bottom, as it were, there's something that's "outside" of death, "outside" of accidents, "outside" of illness.

In other words, the so-called freedom found at the summit of consciousness can also be found in the body.

But it is found in small breaths, as it were, through a thousand little experiences. Because the body is something very slow to learn its own freedom. The body doesn't believe in its freedom—it believes in all its habits. It believes in all the diseases; it believes in the whole medical catalog: "If I do this, such and such thing will happen." Our entire world —the world we live in—is a world of laws, of cause and effect, constantly: "If I do this, such and such a thing will happen."

We don't realize the extent to which we are PHYSIOLOGI-CAL prisoners.

We might realize we are the prisoner of an idea, of a feeling, of a sensation, but we don't know that . . . in fact, we are PHYSIOLOGICALLY a prisoner.

And that freedom is possible.

When we manage to get through all those successive layers of conditioning, we attain a freedom which is in the body's depths. We suddenly escape the Law—the so-called Law in which biologists confine us. All of a sudden, something else emerges.

> TOWARNICKI: *You wrote that man is a prisoner in a sort of "fishbowl."*

Yes.

> TOWARNICKI: *And that one has to break that fishbowl?*

Yes.

We think that the beyond of man lies either in a dissolution of the body (when we go into the Spirit, so-called), or in a perfection of the present instrument, leading to a . . . superfish in its fishbowl, with eventually a few more dorsal fins or some new, fabulous tool.

But the truth is, we are inside a bowl, and the other side of the bowl is not death. And one doesn't get outside the bowl by improving the instruments that belong to the inside of the bowl.

One day, around the Paleozoic era, some fish found themselves in drying-up waterholes and, out of necessity, they HAD to learn a different mode of breathing, to move from gill respiration to pulmonary respiration.

They had—since they were more and more asphyxiated— they had to find another way of breathing. And the amphibians were born. They left the fishbowl. They left THEIR bowl to find that the other side of the bowl was not death; it was merely another way of breathing.

The end of the fish is not death. It's another species, which is amphibian, which breathes a different air.

Similarly, all the way down at the bottom of the PSEUDO-physiology we know—which is not the real body, but simply an IDEA of the body, a HABIT of the body, the fishbowl where we are confined—at the bottom of that, we break the . . . glass wall confining us and we move into another . . . (what shall I say? . . . It isn't "another world," any more than the amphibian landed in another world), we emerge into another MATERIAL air, another mode of breathing . . . IN MATTER.

Another Law.

Clearly, what presides over the bird and what presides over the fish are two very radically different laws. Well, once we break this fishbowl—not illusorily at the summit of consciousness, but in the very depths of the body—once we pierce through all those layers of conditioning, we really, MATERIALLY, PHYSIOLOGICALLY emerge into another . . . POSSIBILITY OF BEING—IN A BODY.

TOWARNICKI: *And we reach, as Mother said, what is called "the cellular consciousness."*

Yes—the cellular consciousness, which is a cellular "power" and a cellular "vision." It's an entirely new WAY OF BEING in matter. Where death no longer has any power. Where accidents no longer have any power. Where the vision is different.

It's a whole . . . new and different WAY OF BEING coming to life, which Mother stammered out, tried to explain to me day after day, for nineteen years.

I listened to her for nineteen years.

And every time, those experiences were dizzying for her. When you abruptly find yourself outside of the bowl or outside the network of the web, it's quite "bewildering," quite distressing for the old physiology, for the old way of doing things. At first, it looks a little like madness. Many people around Mother thought she was becoming unhinged. It's very eccentric to get out of the human skin and try a . . . new way of being.

What did the old fish say when facing the first amphibian? And what did the old Paleozoic reptile say when facing the first archeopterix? He must have said, "This is impossible! He's crazy! It's an hallucination! It's impossible, it's impossible, it's impossible."

So our entire material world, including that of the disciples around Mother, was constantly saying, "It's impossible, it's impossible. . . ."

And in all this, I was the one (I now realize), the one who said, "Yes, it's possible! It's possible; it's the ONLY possibility." Because deep down in me was—it's not faith, rather a certain profound way of breathing—this certitude: "But OF COURSE, it's possible! It's even the ONLY possibility! We've had enough of the Upanishads, enough of the Vedas and the . . . Bibles, and Marxism and all the old human stories—we must find a NEW MODE OF BREATHING."

And that's where I plunged with Mother—plunged, well, I was there . . . truly like a drowning old man desperately trying to . . . find the OTHER way of breathing.

99

Mother's Exploration: An Ubiquitous Consciousness, the New Physics

TOWARNICKI: *Mother used to speak of speed, of radiation, of light, of "lightning-fast waves."*

I would like to try to explain, in simple terms, what that other state may be like. Actually, it isn't something we don't know anything about. It isn't something at all foreign to man. Children would be capable of feeling it or experiencing it. And quite a few adults have known that other state (without being aware of it).

For there are moments in life when, all of a sudden, you are invincible—absolutely nothing can touch you. If you are on a battlefield, you feel you can go through a hail of bullets unharmed. If you are in the middle of a storm at sea, you laugh and you know that, somehow, you'll make it through those enormous waves. Assassins are sent to kill you, and something in you remains so PERFECTLY still, as if the whole thing were a comedy—they couldn't possibly touch you. And the assassins actually can't touch you.

In one form or another, a lot of people have had this experience: you are suddenly outside the "Law." You are outside all that seems inevitable—you slip through the meshes. And all those who've had this experience report that there's a sort of . . . not exactly exhilaration, but like a shot of adrenaline, and you are suddenly filled with invincible energy. Something very simple and very joyous. But mainly very simple. A kind of childlike guilelessness that says, "No, no, no, no, no. It's impossible; this accident can't happen."

Well, there you have already an indication of the other state. In other words, for a few seconds, those beings who've had this kind of experience have slipped through the layers of conditioning, the fears, the "this or that will happen," the "this is possible, that's impossible"—for a few seconds of grace, they've slipped through the web, and so nothing touches them. Nothing can touch them.

That's what the experience is.

In other words, after breaking through all those evolutionary layers, you suddenly EMERGE, in the depths of the body, into something where the old laws of the world NO LONGER have power. And you realize that their power was nothing but a huge collective suggestion—and an OLD habit. But JUST a habit.

There are no "laws"; there are only fossilized habits.

And the whole process is to break through those habits.

So sometimes, in a human life, there are a few seconds when one feels: "Ah, I've slipped through!"

But that state has to come to a point when it's experienced spontaneously and naturally by the body, which means freeing it of all its conditioning. Then you emerge into something fantastic. But *really* fantastic! . . . Although I suppose that the first gliding of a bird in the air also was fantastic. Yet there was a moment when an old reptile took off and became a bird.

You see, the next step in evolution has nothing to do with creating super-philosophies, super-Beethovens or superelectronic machines. It has to do with finding PHYSIOLOGICALLY —because evolution is physiological—finding physiologically a NEW STATE IN MATTER—not in the pure Spirit.

But then, you notice something quite extraordinary with the body (in fact, maybe with all life), which is that the obstacle IS the lever: To find a wall, to know there is a wall, is to be able to break through it.

Medical science and biology have "codified" the obstacles— they have crystallized and made the obstacles into laws—

while they are only means. They are levers. If there's a wall, it means there's another side to the wall. If there's an impossibility, there's a possibility. It can't be any other way. And so the greatest difficulty is to find out WHERE the wall is.

But all those obstacles—those illnesses which appear to follow an irrevocable course, death, gravity, each and every one of our laws, so carefully codified and set as an obstacle, that is, as the indefeasible limits of our bowl—are, in fact, means.

If you PRESS against the obstacle (you have to press against it), if you press against the obstacle instead of . . . instead of taking things naturally; if life STOPS being natural as you know it, if you pursue the obstacle everywhere, you can overcome it.

And that's what Mother did. Anytime there was a Law, an Impossibility—for her that "law," or that "impossibility" did not exist. And it's because she had the courage to break through all those . . . formidable imperatives, you know, which WEIGH on the body's consciousness—all the obstacles, the "You can't do this," all that swarming death with its attractive medical masks—it's because she had the courage to break through all that, to PRESS against all the obstacles, that she eventually got through, only to realize that the so-called laws were just our . . . way of mapping out a certain fishbowl, and that on the other side lay another possibility of being.

Then you find deep inside in the body something . . . very similar—surprisingly similar—to what you find at the summit of consciousness, in the great expanses, at the apex of the being—but you find it physiologically, cellularly.

The body is made of matter.

And what is matter?

We think it's limited to a particular body, but it isn't so! Scientists know this. Matter is a continuum; there is no separation anywhere. An electromagnetic wave is everywhere at once, in everything.

And so Mother's body began to experience truly fantastic things, which she confided to me because she knew I didn't think her crazy. She felt she COULD talk to me, while she couldn't say a word to the others. She could, because she knew that, having experienced the . . . asphyxiation I had experienced, for me EVERYTHING was possible. Or I WANTED everything to be possible.

And so, in the depths of that "pure" cellular consciousness, free of its coverings, we begin to touch upon really fantastic things—materially fantastic—which in fact parallel many discoveries of modern physics.

In particular, we realize that the body's consciousness is not IN THE LEAST confined to a particular body; it is everywhere at once. We are the ones who are confined in an illusory physiology. When we come into contact with that cellular consciousness deep inside the body, there's no longer "one body"; all at once . . . the whole world is there.

So Mother used to have fantastic experiences. There were things happening in New York, in Paris, in New Delhi and everywhere, and she was THERE—she was there PHYSICALLY. The consciousness OF HER BODY (it wasn't the vision of a psychic, experienced through the so-called third eye), it was the body that . . . communicated at once with everything.

There is a cellular consciousness that isn't confined. Matter as . . . even as physicists see it, isn't confined—it's in motion, in perfect continuity with everything. That body is suddenly without boundary! It KNOWS everywhere. It IS everywhere. It LIVES everywhere. It's a sort of ubiquitous consciousness.

It is at once fascinating and dangerous to talk of these fantastic experiences, because they're in fact something far simpler than we think.

The next being is not a second-rate actor.

It is difficult to describe that simplicity on an earthly scale. But it can be EXPERIENCED. And that's what Mother tried to convey—convey to me.

It can be experienced.

At that moment, you see, there's no longer . . . no longer any sense of a little "I," a little human ego with its "powers" and fantastic "visions."

The cellular consciousness is a childlike consciousness. It's very guileless. It's . . . exceedingly simple. It's the original simplicity of the world. So it goes through everything and finds itself "at home" in everything: in a blade of grass, in the wind, and especially in suffering, in much of the terrible suffering of this world. It's painful.

To be sure, there are fantastic aspects to this. To feel that we are a mountain, a river, a forest—all that is . . . grandiloquent. Indeed, there is a certain simplicity that causes us to be everywhere, to be a part of everything, one with everything. . . . Why? Because as there is only one Matter, there is only one Consciousness.

But that Consciousness of oneness is not to be found on a small point of being disappearing into somnolent bliss. It is to be found in a total physical identity in which . . . not only do you participate in everything, but you ARE everything—you breathe with everything. You are in the same heartbeat with everything that is.

And you are one and the same pain with many pains.

TOWARNICKI: *She perceived waves?*

She didn't "perceive" (it sounds absurd to say it this way); she WAS like lightning-fast waves, everywhere, instantaneous, so fast that they were as if absolutely still.

Here, we are truly entering a new kind of physics. And the first change in that new physics is that the very sense of TIME is different. We live at a speed . . . that is not the speed we are used to.

(short silence)

That consciousness (the consciousness of the body, that is), instantaneously extending to the entire physical continuum, does not travel at the regular human speed—there's a different sense of time.

Thus, we understand that, if we are capable of LIVING in that other "time," or at that other speed, the old law of the body is altered: the wear and tear associated with time no longer exists. We are no longer 82 years old + 1 day + 2 days + 3 days. Another physiology begins to . . . emerge—a new mode of BEING begins to emerge.

But . . . that's where we begin to measure not only the perils and sheer madness of such an attempt—to move on to a new species—but also the great pain of such an experience. Because to emerge into the world's physical oneness—physiological oneness—is to enter the world's "total" misery, as it were.

And with her customary humor (because there was always that humor, in everything she did), Mother used to say, "It's like constantly catching a new illness and having to find a cure for it."

She caught thousands and thousands of illnesses. She constantly had . . . blank seconds. From one second to the next, it's as though she were face to face with death. Not just her own death, but the death of a disciple, the death of this person, the suffering of that person. So at each second, she had to bring in that new oxygen, as it were, or that new Law, to overcome the flash-illness or flash-death suddenly seizing her. She would stop. She would go completely white. And . . . something else—something of the other Law—would come in and counteract, overcome the obstacle of that suffering.

It's very difficult to put these things into words, but it's as if Mother actually worked on the entire body of the earth. She no longer was a body confined within a particular skin.

Perhaps we can understand the dimension of the experience by its mental analogy: when we emerged from the primates and began to "think" and "communicate" a little, that new consciousness began to EMBRACE a lot of things.

In a sense, to understand means TO BE INSIDE what one understands. It's truly like embracing it.

And so the more refined the human being becomes and the more he widens his consciousness, and the more he communicates, the more things he "takes in"—the more things he embraces. Hence a more refined person is often one who suffers, because he understands a lot of things—he embraces a lot of things. One can certainly grasp this mental dimension of the process, but it is in the body that the "understanding," that special way of embracing things, took place. It took place in the consciousness of the body. That is, Mother's body embraced many sufferings in order to work on them—to work on that falsehood, the enormous falsehood that illness is, that suffering is, that pain is, that death is. And by filtering a new . . . kind of oxygen into her body, she filtered it into the body of the world, as it were. A few drops of something else that . . . altered the density or heaviness of things.

And this is where the phenomenon becomes extremely interesting, when one can appreciate it.

The first reaction of a body when given, say, a new kind of oxygen or a new kind of food—when faced with conditions other than those it is used to—is panic. Instant fear: everything starts to boil and bubble, to fall apart, to become disorganized.

But this is exactly what has been happening in the world body for the last twenty years! There's a feeling that everything is going awry, falling apart. Nothing works as it used to—nothing is natural anymore. It's as if our entire mental system were completely rotten, as it were, and there's no solution to anything. All the truths are falling to pieces. All the falsehoods masquerade as truths. There's a feeling of living in a world that's . . . completely coming apart.

But why? Why is that so?

It may just well be that a new Law, a new air, is filtering into the old human bowl and beginning to BREAK the meshes. So we cry for help. We are outraged: "What's happening is just awful!"

But what is actually happening?

It's just that the meshes are breaking apart. And they're breaking apart everywhere in the world. Not because evil is coming out, or because truth (as we conceive it) is coming out. But because there's truly a new air, a new oxygen, slipping in and UPSETTING everything—driving everything out of its false naturalness, out of its false good as well as its false evil.

And absolutely everything is breaking down, you see! The truths as well as the falsehoods. Nothing remains standing anymore. But, look, when the first saurian or first reptile had to let go of its body and grow wings because the world was becoming suffocating—what happened? Something

107

must have been shattered inside that reptile's skin. It must have been horribly painful to be inside that saurian skin when it had to grow wings. Or even inside that fish, when it had to evolve from gill respiration to another mode of respiration. It's suffocating to evolve to "another." It's excruciating. Everything is shattered, torn apart.

The entire Earth body is being torn apart.

That's what is happening now.

So if we believe that we are moving toward new unities, new worldwide fraternities, that we shall save the poor and make a better society, we are sorely mistaken, you see. We are not going to make better fish—we are in the process of making a new species.

And then—at last—perhaps we will realize that that Spirit, that Light, that Joy—what we were seeking at the summit of consciousness, our eyes closed, in silence and retreat—lies in matter itself, that it *is* matter itself, and that such was the purpose of those thousands of years of suffering. We went from one cataclysm to another to force us gradually to discover our own secret—our secret IN MATTER.

But not that of the biologists, not that of the physicists, not that of the old code, that is, the old dogmas. Our physical dogmas are as irrelevant as our religious dogmas. We have to emerge into something else. And we are IN THE PROCESS of emerging into something else through all this chaos.

So there's a hope—not just a hope, it's even tangible—that what one dreamed of as a child on the seashore, what seemed so . . . at once so vast and so part of ONESELF, you know . . . When I looked at the sea, it wasn't something "else"—that little wave wasn't something else. I flowed with it, I . . . rippled with that little wave. I was that smell of seaweed. . . . It wasn't something else, something other!

108

At the end of all that suffering, we can find, in the body, what we knew as a child, and what we knew also on the summits of meditation. Then matter takes on its own meaning.

The purpose of evolution is not to get out of it. The purpose of matter is not to give it up—it is to find its true secret. And its true secret has nothing to do with electronics. It has to do with a Joy in matter, a Consciousness in matter, a Power in matter that will enable us to LIVE differently, a truly divine life on earth.

But we have to use the right means, UNDERSTAND the process. We have to understand that all the chaos we are going through right now is not the bankruptcy of civilization, not the bankruptcy of morality, not the bankruptcy of religion—it's nothing like that. It's the bankruptcy of the old fish in order to MOVE ON to its next plenitude.

Then everything has meaning.

TOWARNICKI: *But what about those who feel a malaise and who live in Paris, London, Buenos Aires or anywhere? How can they take this path?*

But . . . you don't "take" this path! You live it, actually, at every minute of the day! And you can live it everywhere: in London, in Paris—and, I think, far more intensely when you are in the midst of this horrible thing.

Suffocation is the means itself.

Like the old reptiles, we are faced with increasingly suffocating circumstances in order for . . . for humanity to open its mouth and call, cry out. There's no way to evolve into something else unless there's a NEED to evolve into something else. That's obvious.

TOWARNICKI: *You think that the modern world is show-ing, revealing its own limits?*

They are being shattered everywhere, the limits.

The limits of horror as well as the limits of good—all the limits are being broken to pieces, shattered. To an impartial observer this world appears to be completely mad. It appears mad in its good as much as in its evil. Clearly, something ELSE is trying to come into the picture. And that suffocation is palpable to all people a bit sensitive, whether they live in London, Washington or anywhere—you'd have to be made of a very rudimentary stuff not to feel it. But that suffocation is a means, because when you suffocate, you have to find the MEANS of getting out of it.

And what is the means?

It is exceedingly simple, you see. It is only to call. When you are stifled, you call for air.

That's all it takes.

The Purpose of Science,
The Cry of the Next Species

TOWARNICKI: *When someone sets out on this path, what impressions does he have of the modern technical world, the world of information, communications?*

Ah, for me it absolutely looks like—I'm sorry—superfish in their fishbowl contriving elaborate antennae and fins and claws and . . . It seems so . . . so childish, so narrow!

They are so totally beside the point. And it's because they're hopelessly beside the point that . . . that a grace is at work to break them despite themselves. That's what the grace does: it breaks down everything. Otherwise, left to our own humanity, we would ENDLESSLY create superelectronic gadgets and superfins . . . until we eventually cut our own throat, you see. But something is in the process of mercilessly breaking all that to pieces.

TOWARNICKI: *You said that . . .*

And it will happen! The breakdown will happen, the general breakdown of their wonderful system.

Then we'll see how man wakes up to . . . what kind of eye he will open when faced with the breakdown of his enormous machinery. What kind of eye will he open when nothing works anymore?

I think all those electronic and mechanical powers are being given extraordinary proofs of their powerlessness. We need only to remember America struggling with the problem of a few hostages in Iran to realize the impotence of that enormous power.

Indeed, our enormous power is totally impotent.

That's what we are in the process of finding out—progressively.

TOWARNICKI: *You said that the more we talk about information, the less informed we are. The more perfect and sophisticated the means of communications appear to be, the less we really communicate.*

Actually, the real purpose of science is not to have invented all those "gadgets"; it isn't to have produced superjets. Its REAL CONTRIBUTION (if one could step back and have a bird's-eye view of history) is to have woven such a dense and tight network among all the parts of the globe, all the groups of humanity, to have created such a unity, such an inextricable network, that you can't do the slightest thing in a remote corner of France without its having repercussions in Washington or Beijing. Everything is tied together in a single unity. You can't do a thing or move a finger here without its moving everywhere.

This is the true purpose of science.

It has woven this humanity into a kind of unity—DESPITE ITSELF—a unity so compact that either we make it together or we perish together.

In other words, science has been an instrument of global awareness. What used to be the privilege of a few individuals in their remote castles, Himalayas or Egyptian temple . . . is now perceived and experienced by humanity as a whole. There is a single human bundle and we all must find . . . the way out.

We must find the solution.

Indeed, a new species is not made by a single individual. A new species means that the whole moves on to the next species together. The whole moves on to a new dimension. It isn't just one individual. . . . Evolution is not meant for a privileged few; it's meant for a human totality. If we are to move to another stage, we ALL do it. We all move there together!

So the purpose of that science was not to provide us with all those gadgets. It was, rather, to tie us into one human bundle so we can find together, or CALL together—CALL together. When things become suffocating enough, you see, when that web gets more and more stifling, more and more stifling, there comes a moment when something inside us really CRIES OUT—it cries, "Something else, something else! I need something else! Enough of this! Something else!"

And that's when the miracle may happen (what we call a miracle). Just like the cells, when they are seized with a

great, serious illness—all of a sudden, they start calling
from deep inside the body and, pfft, the illness is dissolved!

Well, if the earth's body, faced with its own death, lets out
that cry of appeal, something can happen and . . . change
everything.

We are at that moment. We are getting closer and closer
to the moment when millions—not just a few—millions and
millions of beings will have to utter the cry of the new
species—the cry of appeal.

TOWARNICKI: *Yet death got the better of Mother. She
died.*

That's . . . something else again.

The Crooks

TOWARNICKI: *You are talking of your own experience. Do
you have friends, perhaps disciples? . . .*

Oh, no! *(laughter)* No! Lord, no! Certainly not!
Disciples of what?

Disciple is a word I could never understand. One LOVES
something. One NEEDS something. So, yes, I am a disciple
of the sun, I am a disciple of the sea, I am a disciple of the
open air, I am a disciple of what's beautiful. Yes.

But no disciples.

I'm sorry, I interrupted you.

TOWARNICKI: *Not at all. I wanted to talk about what
happened after Mother left. When you speak of your
experience, of Mother's experience, of Sri Aurobindo's
message, do you expect much of those who listen to*

you? Are you severe in your judgment of them?

Severe? Oh, no! If there's something I can't be . . . Be severe? What's the sense of it?

I was surrounded by so much severity as a child.

To be severe means that one does not understand. The more one understands, the more one loves—the more one loves.

Where is weakness? Where is incapacity? Where is wrong-doing, error? These are things I don't understand. I don't understand them.

The only thing that . . . for which I may, indeed, be quite severe, that I really can't stomach, is cheaters, phonies. Those I don't accept.

TOWARNICKI: *I think I should put my question differently. I meant: Satprem signifies "The One Who Truly Loves."*

Yes.

TOWARNICKI: *It's the name Mother gave you.*

Yes.

TOWARNICKI: *But can one always truly love?*

I would almost say that it's a question of temperature.

What does it mean, to love?

What does it mean, to understand?

It means being INSIDE . . . things, beings; it means perceiving what they are. It means feeling, through one mask or another, the heart that's there—the kind heart. Human

114

beings have a kind heart. They don't know it, in fact.

I don't know, but out of a hundred people I might meet, ninety-nine have a kind heart; they have forgotten the child that they are, but they remain that child at heart—a child looking out at the sun and smiling at God knows what. One can touch that behind all the masks. It's what I feel, I touch, and that's what I love. I love that because I "am" with that.

Though sometimes, certain so-called human beings garb themselves, dress themselves up in ideas, light, spirituality, this and that, while there is just a nasty, selfish MUCK in them, something that wants to take—something predatory.

Then I am severe.

Those are really the ones who have betrayed their humanity.

Then I am not afraid of using the sword.

Then I am merciless.

The crooks, you know.

And those crooks are found mainly (not among the wretched or the outcasts, not among the wicked or the vicious—that's not where they are found), mainly among those beings who have seized the truth, who are all dressed in white and . . . display a great spirituality, while behind they have claws and only want to take.

That's . . . disgusting.

The phonies of the Spirit, you know—the cheats.

TOWARNICKI: *You are thinking about the growing number of false gurus. . . .*

Yes, some of them are like that.

I was thinking about the ashram.

But then again, even in this case, one never knows, because through those false gurus and false spiritualists, all

115

those phonies, well, someone may just grasp something. Sometimes, as Mother said, one reaches the goal faster through a devil than through a god.

If you are sincere—despite the false guru—the false guru himself will bring you into contact with exactly what you need. Then you will go beyond it.

So even those crooks are hard to nail, because if they are still around, it may mean that they have their purpose? One meets every necessary foe.

So I really don't know at what . . . point, what place, what line, you start condemning. I'm not sure there is anything at all to condemn.

One can't make general rules, you see. If I meet a phony, I tear off his mask . . . mercilessly.

TOWARNICKI: *Has it happened?*

Yes, it has happened. If I am alive today, it isn't my fault!

But what can you say. . . . Those are negative things. They are individual.

They are not the kind of things to be given as a model. The only thing is to have enough genuine love in one's heart in order to recognize it wherever it is. And that genuine love is also a power. If it must destroy, it destroys. But that is an individual law; it isn't something you can give as a model.

As you mentioned so rightly, in her present appearance, India gives the impression of an immense falsehood—an enormous falsehood. And all the more enormous as it is garbed in spirituality.

The old idols had to be broken.

We must regain the truth that we ARE deep down. But that truth that we ARE in the depths can only be reached after we break the falsehood within ourselves.

True, India has a very corrupt appearance, but perhaps it is because her idols are too old and fossilized, and she has to rediscover what she really is.

There too, in India, things are falling apart, as in the rest of the world, in order to get to . . . what is.

Free Matter

The Vedic Rishis

TOWARNICKI: *How is traditional Indian spirituality—Buddhism, Hinduism—expressed today?*

SATPREM: Well, it's always the same thing. They all practice meditation. They all withdraw from appearances or activity, and they try to come into contact with another depth of consciousness. And that's it. That's the old story. It has been going on for . . . thousands of years.

But where is their solution?

Where is India today, with all its spiritual powers?

It's one of the most corrupt countries in the world. Instead of INCARNATING the truth, the way the ancient rishis did, instead of driving that truth down into the body, they have chosen to cut themselves off in nice little meditations. So life has continued its round unchecked, while self-interest and machinery took over Indian matter—because they neglected matter. And now they have to rediscover the potent truth behind that crust of falsehood.

TOWARNICKI: *Could we say that, beyond Buddhism—*

Yes.

TOWARNICKI: *—the source from which Sri Aurobindo, Mother or yourself have drawn is very close to the teaching of the Vedas, the rishis?*

Ah, they may be the only ones (at least that we know of)! The rishis knew "that." They knew the truth in the depths of matter, what they called "the sun in the darkness."

The atom is a sun—a sun covered over by a great darkness. The rishis knew that.

But if the rishis of five, six, seven thousand years ago had truly discovered and incarnated the secret, well, evolution, human evolution, would never have taken place! The secret couldn't have been discovered by a few rishis on their mountaintop. It has to be discovered—won—by humanity as a whole.

Again, evolution is not the business of a privileged few. There are forerunners—the rishis were forerunners.

At the beginning of an experience, a civilization or a cycle there are always those who are harbingers, who trace the curve of an entire age, the trajectory—who foresee the course and say, "This is what will happen. This is the goal." And after that, the actual course has to be traveled, you see, so that it is no longer the experience of one small individual but of a whole species.

In the past, it was the experience of a privileged civilization. Now, it isn't even a matter of civilization anymore. It's one SINGLE human bundle that has to undergo the experience.

TOWARNICKI: *The rishis were the Vedic priests who lived before Buddha. . . .*

Yes, the rishis were . . . warriors, primarily. They lived about seven thousand years ago, as far as we can tell. It was well before Buddhism. Buddhism dates back five hundred years before Christianity. It was well before the Upanishads, which are already a rather distorted form of the Vedas—they are already the beginning of the intellectual cycle.

The Vedas have the secret. They stammer it. They give some hints of it in imagery.

(short break)

It is hard to appreciate the incredible revolution that Sri Aurobindo's and Mother's discovery represents.

You see, everything is devalued in our world. Things have been so overinflated—all kinds of little things have been so overinflated—that nothing seems to make sense anymore. Our mental world is extremely devalued. That's the most enormous devaluation of all.

But truly, Mother's and Sri Aurobindo's discovery is . . . There hasn't been anything more important since the appearance of ORIGINAL LIVING MATTER.

It's a change in the Law of original living matter.

I am not sure people can fully appreciate what that means.

And I would like to return again to that process of descent into the body.

I wish people could actually grasp the PRACTICAL secret, the "why it's POSSIBLE," when all biology tells us, "It isn't possible."

This is what biologists say: "The sequence of amino acids determines once and for all whether you will be a human being, a mouse or a giraffe. If they are wound this way, you will inescapably produce a mouse; if they are wound in a slightly different way, you will inescapably produce human proteins or giraffe proteins." And there's no way out of this. Except through accident, some accidental radiation, which will produce monsters.

So, imagine, if one human being truly found the "passage," as the Vedic rishis called it, the way out of this predicament—and not into Nirvana, you see—the way out into a matter that will . . . really be what it is. Because we don't know what matter really is.

In fact, if we consider human thought since its origin— what we know of its origin—we realize that there has been a tremendous (how shall I put it?) degradation or "decay" of the original truth or original discovery made by the Vedic rishis (to go back only to them, because there may have been others before).

TOWARNICKI: *Four thousand years ago?*

At least. At least four thousand years ago. It's more likely to be five, six, or even seven thousand years. Because for a long long time, what they said, the mantras they chanted, was repeated by word of mouth—and how long did that last? We have no idea.

Truly, if you take some of those texts from the Rig-Veda, which are really the most ancient texts known to humanity, you realize that those people had a secret, and a secret in matter.

I don't know, I have here some of those texts from the Rig-Veda, and they are . . . full of light.

They say this (in the Rig-Veda): "That which is immortal in mortals . . . is established inwardly as an energy working out our divine powers." And this: "Let us conquer even here, let us run this battle-race of a hundred leadings." And again this, from the Atharva Veda: "I am a son of Earth, the soil is my mother." And this: "May we speak the beauty of thee, O Earth, that is in thy villages and forests and assemblies of war and battles."

The people who uttered these words were certainly not little meditative beings.

And they said even more extraordinary things, if we understand their symbolism. The "Rock" (what they call the Rock or the mountain) is the symbol of matter, of the original terrestrial formation.

This is what they say (still in the Rig Veda): "Our fathers by their words [or mantra, that is, the vibration of a sound, the vibration of consciousness] broke the strong and stubborn places; they shattered the mountain rock with their cry. They made in us a path to the Great Heaven [in other words, in matter—not up above on meditative peaks, but IN matter]. They discovered the sun dwelling in darkness. . . . They found the treasure of heaven hidden in the secret cavern like the young of the Bird, within the infinite rock."

And they again say this: "The contents of the pregnant hill [still matter, the symbol of matter] came forth for the supreme birth. Then, indeed, they awoke and saw all behind and wide around them, then, indeed, they held the ecstasy that is enjoyed in heaven." And finally: "They discovered the well of honey covered by the rock."

So they were people who were aware of a secret in matter.

Something that has nothing to do with the Upanishads or with what has formed the present Indian tradition, for . . . we shouldn't forget that the Upanishads—which came two thousand years later and became the basis and Gospel of all India—say, "Leave this world of illusion. . . . Brahman is real; this world is a falsehood."

That's what the Niralamba Upanishad says.

So you can see the decline, as it were, the degradation. Instead of seeking that "battle-race of a hundred leadings," as the rishis advocated, they shut their eyes, crossed their legs—and then salvation is in heaven. Actually, I don't know much about what other mystics have said, but most of them took that ascending path—up and up and up, and they're gone. Heaven is "somewhere out there," beyond death. This is the whole story, the whole DEGRADATION, or loss, of the human secret.

And this is what Sri Aurobindo and Mother found again.

This is why I say there hasn't been a more fantastic discovery since the appearance of the FIRST LIVING MATTER on earth. Because it involves a CHANGE in the very law of that first living matter.

Which means that our entire biology COLLAPSES before that discovery.

The Mind of the Cells

I really would like to try to tell HOW it is possible, in simple terms.

The fantastic discovery was what first Sri Aurobindo found, then Mother, because Mother continued on the path and she rediscovered what Sri Aurobindo had discovered.

They discovered what they called a "mind of the cells."

And that's the fantastic discovery.

Let me try to describe the process in this way:

We all live very far removed from our body, in a small part of our being that we have HORRENDOUSLY cultivated—and very usefully cultivated, too—which is the intellectual mind. You can't do a thing without its being immediately "snatched" by a thought and filed away in a little compartment. This is truly the first of those layers I mentioned earlier which cover us—which HIDE matter's reality from us.

For what, actually, do biologists know of matter's reality? They look at it through a microscope, but what can the microscope tell them? Can they "experience" the cell through a microscope? All they do is draw up a catalog of features; they make an image of the cell—but with what? What is looking through the microscope? It's their MIND that looks through the microscope and makes an image, a projection, of its own mental conception of the cell.

So, first, that intellectual mind has to be silenced.

Then we encounter a second mental layer, which is the emotional mind—all the passions, emotions and all that—which makes quite a considerable covering.

And deeper still. Because as one layer clears up, the next one automatically comes into view. In our normal consciousness, all this is a sort of undifferentiated hodgepodge. Passions take on intellectual appearances; the intellect is used to cover up all kinds of desires; it's a complete hodgepodge. People talk of their "thoughts," their "feelings," but in fact nothing is clear-cut and pure in all that—it's an enormous mixture.

Thus, after going through the intellectual layer, one comes upon that "pure" emotional mind: all the feelings and emotions, all that blurs and colors our perception of the body— all our moods constantly interfere and COLOR the reality of what we might be.

125

So that layer, too, has to be gone through. In other words, all those feelings have to be silenced; those emotions have to be neutralized or "clarified." And that's a real battle. It's really, as the rishis put it, a "battle-race of a hundred leadings," because you cut one off and another one grows right back.

Then, still deeper, when that layer of the emotional mind has been quieted, we find the sensory mind. And all that clothes itself in a particular language; it's an infinitesimal vibration, but nonetheless it expresses itself in a particular language. Here we encounter all the ordinary sensations that form the very fabric of our being.

And if we go right down to the bottom of these sensations, we find what Sri Aurobindo and Mother called the "physical mind."

That is truly like the PRIMARY mind of matter. That is to say, a sort of relentless memory endlessly repeating whatever habit it has acquired. If it bumps into something, it will remember it fifty years later. If it's told, "This will become an illness which may last from 3 to 6 months," it's as if the cells were suddenly imprinted, and you HAVE to be ill for 3 months, you HAVE to be ill for 6 months—you HAVE to. And if it is told, "Take such and such a medicine and you'll recover," the cells very obediently say, "Oh, all right, I'll take that medicine and I'll recover." It's a sort of hypnotism.

And this is where we begin to touch—where Mother and Sri Aurobindo began to touch—the secret. Which is that that primary matter—those cells—is so good-willed—STUPIDLY GOOD-WILLED, as Mother used to say. There are no "laws" for it, just hypnotism and fear. In other words, whatever gets imprinted on that primary cell will be repeated endlessly, with unremitting goodwill.

And, of course, its first imprints are fear, aggression. There is that whole devouring world out there, that teeming, threatening life—life is a cataclysm for the first living matter. It steps out into a cataclysm, which touches off fear in it. Hence a yearning deep down in that cell for that threat and suffering to cease. In other words, deep down in matter, there's a call for death.

TOWARNICKI: *And the fishbowl is formed.*

Yes, it is formed.

Actually, there is a succession of fishbowls, you might say. The flagellate has cultivated its little flagellate habits; the fish has cultivated its little fish habits, because it was in such and such environment; and the bird also has cultivated its bird habits, because it was in another environment. Each species has WOVEN certain habits.

And biologists come and say, "What's happening is the result of certain amino acids having been wound in such and such a way."

But it's NOT TRUE.

The fantastic discovery is that there are no physical "laws." There are physical HABITS, determined by a certain environment.

And those habits, that "stupid goodwill," can be turned ANY WAY WE LIKE. Though, of course, it isn't in our head that we can change matter's habits—if we want to change matter's habits, we must be in touch with matter! We are NEVER really in touch with it. We are only in touch with our mind, our feelings, passions and habits.

How could we possibly be in touch with the cell?

We must first go through all those layers.

127

But this is the point, the fantastic discovery: one can imprint ANY habit on the cell.

Instead of those "catastrophic" habits. . . . For instance, if a little mishap occurs, the cell panics and starts to weave one layer of skin on top of another, and then another and another, and the result is a tumor. Because there was a tiny problem originally, it says, "All right, as usual, I must produce a layer of skin, then a second layer of skin, then a third layer of skin . . ." It creates its tumor. A small accident happened and, stupidly, it fell into its habit: one layer of skin after another . . .

It's just a habit.

But after going through that layer of the physical mind with its fears, apprehensions and . . . all the tiny habits being constantly woven in us—"Oh, this must be cancer," "Oh, this must be death," "Oh, this must be . . ." (it's all microscopic, but engraved nevertheless)—if we can get through that layer, we discover what Mother and Sri Aurobindo called the "cellular mind." That is, a cellular consciousness that can obey A DIFFERENT KIND of stimulation.

TOWARNICKI: *A different program.*

Yes, a different program.

Instead of a mortal and catastrophic program, that cellular mind can obey a solar vibration, a vibration of joy, a vibration of love.

Instead of weaving death, it can weave something else. And without . . . any extraordinary feat of strength on our part—just getting rid of all these layers of habits covering it. There are no "laws"! There is no "death"! We are the ones who WANT laws, who WANT death. But the cell wants nothing. It wants whatever we want!

Thus, an unbelievable freedom is possible, if we are able to establish communication, so to speak, with the cell. If, instead of instilling those catastrophic habits into it, we instill a habit of joy, of space, of wideness.

This is what Mother and Sri Aurobindo called the "mind of the cells." It's truly like the mind of a child. We can inculcate a TOTALLY DIFFERENT life in it, a totally . . . different way of being.

In terms of evolution, things may take a very long time, but the moment that central will of the cell is open to something else, man can be refashioned . . . at will.

(silence)

Actually, Sri Aurobindo said almost nothing about the secret. Because, obviously, talking about it is fairly useless; it has to be experienced. There is a passage, however, where the secret is spelled out, brought to light.

And it's this one. In a letter, I think, he says this:

"And there is too an obscure mind of the body, of the very cells, molecules, corpuscles. Haeckel, the German materialist, spoke somewhere of the will in the atom, and recent science [here Sri Aurobindo is alluding to Heisenberg], dealing with the incalculable individual variation in the activity of the electrons, comes near to perceiving that this is not a figure but the shadow thrown by a secret reality. This body-mind is a very tangible truth; owing to its obscurity and mechanical clinging to past movements and facile oblivion and rejection of the new, we find in it one of the chief obstacles to permeation by the supermind Force [i.e., the next stage, the next energy] and the transformation of the functioning of the body. On the other hand, once effectively converted, it will be one of the most precious instruments for the stabilisation of the supramental Light and Force in material Nature."

That is what Sri Aurobindo said.

By "stabilisation," he means the establishment of a new mode of vibration or being in matter.

Naturally, a number of knowledgeable people will find such a bodily transformation, such a change of program in matter probably impossible.

But they are forgetting one thing, which is that evolution is something PERPETUALLY heretical. There is nothing less orthodox than evolution! It has spent its time SHATTERING impossibilities—what was impossible for the fish became nonetheless possible later.

And with his wonderful humor, Sri Aurobindo imagines a logician, at the beginning of evolution, looking at things—looking at matter. . . .

And this is what he has that logician say:

"When only matter was there and there was no life, if told that there would soon be life on earth embodied in matter, he would have cried out, 'What is that? It is impossible, it cannot be done. What? This mass of electrons, gases, chemical elements, this heap of mud and water and stones and inert metals—how are you to get life in that? Will the metal walk?' "

Will the cells escape their program?

This is the challenge of Mother and Sri Aurobindo.

This is truly the question of our time.

It isn't a philosophical issue anymore, the old story of one civilization following another. . . .

It's really a revolution to be made IN matter.

The Mantra

TOWARNICKI: *But what about the reader, he or she reading these lines, who hasn't been to India, hasn't read Sri Aurobindo, hasn't met Mother—what can they do, if this path interests them?*

Indeed, one CAN consciously do something. Although we must also be aware that the process IS TAKING PLACE, whether we like it or not.

That also is important to know.

That is to say, whether people are conscious of it or not, whether they like it or not, the entire human species is in the process of moving into another evolutionary stage. And that's what is being pounded on every human consciousness, every nation, every group—everywhere. Everything is being broken, broken, broken.

BUT there are people who not only like to understand things but also give their life a real meaning, and who may care to "participate" in that tremendous revolution, which can take place . . . which MUST take place EVERYWHERE.

Evolution is not "Hindu," you see. It must take place, that process must be pursued EVERYWHERE, consciously. Not just when living in special conditions, but in everyday life.

And this is where something so simple can be done, so simple!

What do we do when we walk down the street? What do we do when we ride the elevator? When we go up or down the stairs? What takes place, then, in this human head?

What takes place is a stupid, relentless buzz repeating and repeating, "I have to do this," and "I don't have to do that," and "Maybe this will happen," and "Maybe that won't happen. . . ." It's a kind of DREADFUL routine, which we breathe quite naturally, but which is absolutely dreadful—a machine churning out one thing, another thing, ten thousand things.

Well, this is exactly where we can get a GRIP on the secret. This is exactly where we can BEGIN the work. Because all those so-called useless, buzzing moments when we walk down the street, ride the elevator or go up the stairs could, instead, be filled with a solar, luminous, joyous vibration.

And this is where India can be of help. For this is how Mother found a practical way: she used a mantra.

What is a mantra?

It's a sound.

Everything has a sound. I am sure scientists could even find the sound of a rock.

Everything has a vibration. A plant has a vibration. Each thing has a vibration, which is the vibration inherent in its nature. Fire has a vibration. If we consider the human realm, joy has a certain vibratory quality, and anger has a different quality. Anybody can feel the difference of vibration (even without words) between a state of joy and a state of pain, or a state of anger. And one can also feel (even without words) the difference of vibration between a person in a state of serenity and a person filled with desires. Their vibratory "environment" is not the same.

And in India they have found the science of these sounds or vibrations.

If you know the sound of something, you can reproduce it.

To give forth the sound of something is in a way to create or reproduce it.

Thus, the Indians have a complete science that, through sounds, enables them to reproduce a state of joy, or vibrations of joy, or vibrations of love. They have also used it for terrible, magic ends, for harming, for causing accidents, for sending all sorts of destructive and negative vibrations.

But . . . but there are sounds of joy, of light, of truth, of love—they, too, exist.

And that's what the mantra is.

So nothing could be simpler: a mantra is one, two or three sounds that, in the beginning, can be repeated in one's mind. Instead of constantly letting ourselves be plagued by all that painful racket—it presses on the temples, you know; our life is constantly assailed, and not only do we churn out all those tiny, catastrophic and defeatist ideas, but we actually "attract" catastrophes and illnesses—our thoughts are magnets. So instead of attracting all those catastrophes, what if we caught ourselves every time and "attracted" a vibration of joy, let's say, or well-being? . . .

Thus, we can practice repeating that mantra of a few sounds when we go up the stairs or walk down the street—it can be repeated at each instant. And since matter is in fact very "repetitive," we can begin, in our mind at first, to CHURN OUT a different sort of routine. Thus, our intellectual mind, which is quite stupid in its substance, in its foundation, will begin to repeat the mantra the way it used to repeat its "I didn't lock the door," and "I forgot my scarf," and "I'm going to miss my appointment"—it will repeat the mantra instead.

Then we realize what a marvel matter is! It can take any imprint whatever; instead of repeating all its stupidities, it can just as well repeat joy and beauty.

Then that sound, that vibration, gradually goes deeper and deeper into matter. From the intellectual mind it goes into the heart, then deeper still . . . and finally the vibration fills the entire body. It's as if your being—your body—gradually acquired another density. As if you were filled with another vibration.

And all the old habits . . . gradually lose their hold. We don't fight against them, because it would be endless—kick out a nasty thought or a nasty idea, and it'll be right back thirty seconds later. Whereas as soon as we have caught the right vibration—which is like a vibration of space, of joy, like the bubbling of the sea, the sparkling of the wave breaking on the beach—matter is very happy to start churning it out. And in the end it does it automatically. And . . . (at least, that's what some people experience) even during sleep we catch ourselves (I've caught myself; it can happen to others), my body catches itself repeating the mantra.

Thus, we understand how the so-called law of death, the law of accidents—all those laws—are DISSOLVED by that vibration. For they don't have any "intrinsic" existence in the cells. The cell repeats ANYTHING WE WANT. And it's we who keep attracting illnesses, accidents, death, degradation, decay to ourselves, out of habit, through our sense of the inevitable, the possible, the impossible, etc.

And, finally, a totally different kind of vibration begins to . . . (how can I put it?) "pulsate" in this matter. And this can be done while walking down the street—personally, I've done it everywhere, in every circumstance, in the most banal as well as the most impossible, in places that seemed suffocating, in . . . I've done it EVERYWHERE.

Mother's Departure

TOWARNICKI: *But up until now, as far as we know, nobody has overcome death. And Mother herself, who fought against death in the same way as Sri Aurobindo, died. So what happened?*

First of all, I am not sure that, individually, a single human being can, FOR HIMSELF, overcome the law of death.

One privileged individual doesn't make any sense. It just doesn't. It's an operation that must involve the consciousness of the earth in its entirety.

Well, not necessarily: it is POSSIBLE to escape the law of death. But . . . that's where the problem begins—not problem, but main difficulty.

You see, as the cell gets more and more purified of all its catastrophic and mortal habits—what happens?

What is hard to grasp is that the minute matter is purified of its catastrophic habits, it instantly becomes ALL of matter. There are no more walls, no more separation. The little individual energy, confined in a fishbowl, is no longer a little energy going round and round; it is a tre-men-dous energy— the very one that drives the universe.

And those who have lived with Mother know what that means, at least a little.

She would say to me . . . How many times did she say, "I have to veil myself! I have to veil myself, otherwise it would be unbearable."

That energy is unbearable. It is so tremendously "pure," as it were, and "solar" that, to the defeatist little squirmings in our depths—all that makes up the stuff of our being—it's like aiming a beam of light into a rat hole. Everything starts to wiggle and thrash about. When one was near Mother, all those dark things in the depths of human matter started to suffocate and thrash about, to sense that . . . their term was coming to an end.

So it isn't enough to become the new species.

You ought also not to be killed by the old one.

And here we come to something . . . very painful, which is really the crux of this human misery.

It is that the earth (the ashram was merely a symbolic representation of the earth, representative human beings, some human substance to be transformed, you could say) and all this matter is extremely leery of joy. It is leery of space, of vastness. It very much clings to its grating little habits. It very much clings to its little ideas, little powers, little ways of being—even if they are "yogic." Go and try to remove from people's consciousness that it is not done cross-legged while burning incense sticks in front of a photograph.

So, more and more, they were saying, "She's becoming unhinged. She's old. She's 92, then 93, then 94. And it's taking forever. It's endless."

It's very sad to say, but . . . that's how it was. They had had enough of Mother.

They had had enough.

As for me, it's only because I had reached the END of all possible experiences, from the day I had cried out in the camps. . . . cried out everywhere—I cried out in the forest, I cried out on the roads of India, I cried out . . . truly at the extreme limits of my own humanity, with such a burning call for "something else"—for that vastness, that light, that beauty. I so INTENSELY needed it that, in a way, I was able to "withstand" that power of light. And even when I felt that my whole body was being crushed—because the pressure of that energy was so tremendous, you know—even when I felt that way, I said, "YES! YES! MORE! And still MORE! And even if I must die of it! . . . Let me die this way rather than in the medical way!"

And then I looked at her . . . I looked at her. She was 92, 93, 94 years old. And so alone. Surrounded by so much incomprehension. They would come to see her and plague her with such petty, such trifling problems: "Should I sell my car at such and such a price?" "Should I marry such and

such a woman?" "Should I do this or should I do that? . . ."
They deluged her with letters, with questions, and even with
ill-will: "I've had enough! Enough! (exactly as I used to say
myself at the beginning) Enough! Let me out of here!"

It's very difficult to bear the Truth—the LIVING Truth.
The LIVING Energy.

I looked at her. . . . Those cells, that body, so clear, so
transparent, was constantly absorbing the surrounding ne-
gation, refusal, and even revolt. Each time it's as if those
cells caught a human disease, or perhaps the human disease—THE human disease. And each time she had to purify,
in her own body, all those suggestions, all that ill-will. . . .

And WHO believed?

WHO said, "Mother WILL find the way. Mother WILL go
through it."

Who believed?

She used to tell me, "I have no one here."

I have no one here.

So that being who tried so much for the earth, who sought
so much for the sake of the love and beauty of the earth—and
. . . "I have no one." It was so . . . moving, poignant, you know,
to see her increasingly crushed, if I may say, by the pain of
that human refusal, that human incomprehension.

There I truly loved Mother.

She was grand.

She was heroic.

Then, one day, they closed her door on me.

TOWARNICKI: *Who?*

Her disciples.

I don't know. I don't understand their world; their way of
being escapes me. I couldn't understand it. I couldn't under-

stand all those jealousies. I couldn't understand any of it.

They closed the door on me.

So there was no one left, you see.

Why become immortal?

Why become radiant?

For herself alone?

She who loved the earth so much, who tried so much to give it its own secret of joy—joy in matter, that is. Its secret of vastness, of communication with everything and everyone.

She has gone.

But she has not gone far.

She is there. She is there.

I feel her. She smiles at me. She holds me.

But this is not for myself alone, either. It's so obvious that anybody can call in his heart, in a childlike way, anywhere, in any language. . . . "That" is ready to help us and . . . make us move mountains.

She is there.

If we have the courage of Joy.

TOWARNICKI: *What did she say to you before she died?*

But they closed her door on me six months before.

TOWARNICKI: *But before that, she told you something: "Others will believe me dead . . ."*

Oh, yes!

TOWARNICKI: *Could you tell us the whole sentence?*

"They will believe me dead. You who know, you will tell them. I would tell them myself, but they will not believe me."
That's what she said.
"But they will not believe me."
What did they believe?
That she was old.
Anyway . . .

TOWARNICKI: *What was that revolt all about? Why did they rebel against Mother during those last years?*

The revolt wasn't manifest. It was a muffled rumbling in many people, and especially in her immediate entourage.
Well, it's . . . fairly easy to understand.
For each one she represented an obstacle to his little desire, his little ego, his little power or prestige. . . . Each one felt it as an obstacle.
In fact, one just has to look around: After she left, the squirmings started to break loose. All those little . . . beings athirst for power, for prestige—all dressed in immaculate white—who even tried to lay their hands on *Mother's Agenda*, all the conversations she had had with me, so afraid were they of what she might have told me. They tried everything.
But there's no point in speaking of those negative things.
They'll go—let them go their own way; it doesn't matter.
More than one old orangutan or old primate protested against man. But that didn't prevent man from coming.
Let them return to their spiritual meditation, to their dust.
But what Mother sowed in the earth, with so much suffering—that's irreversible.
And that's what is in the process of . . . You see, the very same squirming we saw and are seeing in the disciples

around her, well, that's what is now squirming everywhere on earth! It's all the little rats coming out of their holes, all the little cockroaches thrashing about, all the cruelties, the horrible things . . . coming out everywhere, as if the sewers had been opened.

Why? . . . It's because there's truly a STUPENDOUS beam of light that's focused here, revealing all the filth in the depths, so it can be gotten rid of. So something else can emerge from the DEPTHS of this matter, from behind those rat nests, or saint nests—so a new air, a new possibility, can emerge.

That's the phenomenon taking place right now. And it's taking place REGARDLESS of what we want or don't want.

So why not with a little of our breath?

For once in evolution, human beings could participate in their own transformation.

Constantly, constantly, Mother's body used to repeat that same vibration, that same mantra.

Anybody can repeat it.

OM NAMO BHAGAVATE

OM NAMO BHAGAVATE

OM NAMO BHAGAVATE

Om Namo Bhagavate

Om Namo Bhagavate

Om Namo Bhagavate

Om Namo Bhagavate

Translating Mother's Mantra

TOWARNICKI: *Can it be translated?*

Actually, what is the universe calling? Or the bird? Or the plant? What are they calling?
What is the whole earth calling? What is a tree calling?
Joy, love, the supreme . . . the supreme "thing" that is.
Well, that's what the mantra is.
It's: "I salute the Supreme Lord . . . or Supreme Joy or Supreme Beauty. That which fills my lungs. That which fills me, which fills the earth, which makes it grow—I salute the Supreme Lord."

TOWARNICKI: *That's the translation of the mantra?*

Yes. But these are words from our intellect, whereas . . .
That's a translation of our intellect. But this is the vibration, the sound, that needs to be DRIVEN into the body.

TOWARNICKI: *It literally means "Supreme Lord"?*

Supreme Lord.
"Lord" is still . . . our Western translation.
It's the "Bhagavate."
"Bhagavate" is . . . *(laughing)*—is what? What can one say?
It's the breath of everything.
But the TRUE breath—the one we are in fact lacking.

TOWARNICKI: *This is not the same thing. On the one hand, there is the apex of a hierarchic order and the notion of a God creator and driver.*

Oh, yes! Yes, that is still our childlike way of looking at things!

But what is there in the world?

There is only ONE thing. And that's everything that is: it's we, it's you, it's the carpet, it's the chair, it's atoms, it's the galaxies—it's . . . everything that is.

TOWARNICKI: *So one could say "the Supreme Being" or "the Being"?*

"The Being." Yes. That's it.

Yes, "I salute the Supreme Being."

TOWARNICKI: *And even "Supreme" is . . .*

Indeed! Not a Supreme (as Mother says), not a Supreme out of reach! He is here! He is here!

TOWARNICKI: *Precisely.*

It beats in our chest.

It's in each thing, in everything that is. It's in the poor fellow who has reached rock bottom. It's in everything that is.

TOWARNICKI: *So we still haven't translated the mantra.*

Yes. It's a way of breathing.

Oh, all we can do is put a mental or intellectual translation on it.

Actually, it doesn't need any translation—it just needs to vibrate!

And that vibration is full of sunshine.

TOWARNICKI: *Ever since Plato, reason has attempted— because reason is a difficult business and this is not to question the goodwill or capacity of Western thinkers and others who have tried to solve the enigmas—to organize the universe hierarchically, in a mythic form with Plato, or in a theological form through Christianity. Everywhere we see the introduction and establishment of a supreme Mover before which all other creatures are essentially in a state of dependence . . .*

Yes, dependence . . .

TOWARNICKI: *. . . And there only remains for the small movers to salute the big Mover . . .*

Yes . . .

TOWARNICKI: *. . . And that does the trick. We have gone through a whole history of this kind of mental construction, from Scholastism to Platonism to the scientific representation. It is a very sticky problem, because the worth or strength of these approaches is not in question, but they do reveal that a certain narrow and limited type of representation has forever pursued us. As much in the ancient religions and their theological constructions as—*

Yes, but . . .

TOWARNICKI: *—in our Scholastism and our science and technology, which all proceed in the same way.*

Listen, personally I haven't seen anything simpler than these words by the Vedic rishis. They say: "The well of honey covered by the rock."

Towarnicki: *This is still the "withdrawal" envisioned by the Greeks, by Heraclitus and Parmenides, whom we talked about earlier. . . .*

That's what is not covered up.
And that well of honey is there in the depths of everything.
Actually, it is everything.
But we are not yet what we are.
We think of ourselves as a scientist, a monkey, a fish. We think of ourselves as Christian, Buddhist, Hindu. We think of ourselves as lots of things: a giraffe, a little dog. . . . We think of ourselves as lots of things.
While, in fact, we are that honey, that well of honey, covered up by all sorts of habits—of fish, of man, of scientist, of biologist or Christian.
But beneath those habits is something bursting with honey and sunshine, which is what we are.
We can call it "the Supreme," or just "supreme," but that's a poor mental translation.
So when Mother invokes . . . when she salutes that "Bhagavate," she doesn't mean a God, of course!
It's the very being of the world.
But its TRUE being. The one a child knows quite well—without mystery and theology.
So: "I salute that well of honey."

Towarnicki: *What is the translation of the mantra. I am sorry, I have to have it.*

Well, I tried in a thousand ways, or five or six thousand ways, to give a translation, but they are all so poor! But the essence of Mother's mantra is just this: to salute what we ARE—what we aspire to.

What do we aspire to? We aspire to what we are! If we weren't it, we wouldn't aspire to it. If the night were PURELY night, how could it aspire to the sun? How could it aspire to the sun unless it already knew that sun?

TOWARNICKI: *We still don't have a translation!*

The first translation we can give is the mental translation. That is, literally: "I salute That which is supreme."[1]

But that "supreme" is obviously not a celestial Supreme—that is the opposite of the path followed by Mother or the Vedic rishis or Sri Aurobindo.

It's what matter really is.

We have looked for it up above—and we have called it "the Spirit." But the goal of the discovery is to realize that what is all the way up above is RIGHT HERE in matter—that it is matter itself.

That it is the JOY of what is.

How would all this be at all possible if there wasn't a Joy in the depths of everything?

So it is "Supreme Joy."

"I salute Supreme Joy."

---

1. Literally, *Bhagavate* means that which is full, that which is plenitude. According to tradition, the six qualities of *Bhaga* are wealth, heroism, greatness, harmony, knowledge, detachment.

You Can't Assassinate Thin Air

I Walk

TOWARNICKI: *Satprem, sometimes you give the impression of asserting certain things as if they were facts. Aren't you, at times, engaging in a profession of faith? Aren't these things, in fact, mainly hypothetical, merely possibilities? Where is the certitude?*

SATPREM: Oh, yes! . . . Certitude—it's just another way of burning.

Hypothetical? I don't know. It's a particular way of breathing.

Assert? But I don't know! I just walk.

And . . . that's all. I walk and walk and . . . actually I am, rather, a living "question." I am not really interested in answers, in fact—especially when they are mental. What I am interested in is . . . to LIVE or BREATHE or WALK in a certain way that has a broad, harmonious rhythm. Then I feel at ease with myself and I say, "This is the truth" (for me!). In other words, I have touched something true (for me!), because I breathe easily and things unfold with a rhythm.

But aside from that, what is there to assert? I don't know.

I think I have never been able to assert anything in my life. Except that I needed something else. And the nearer one gets to that something else, the more it moves ahead. In other words, there's constant progression.

It's a growing fire.

And where is the fact of the fire?

It's more and more fire, that's all.

TOWARNICKI: *What you are seeking, what Mother sought —is it something one really finds, or it is an unending quest?*

Nothing can ever be definitive.

There is certainly a first step, as it were, when we move from a certain hemisphere of existence into another. Indeed, there is truly a fundamental step when, all of a sudden, we enter another dimension. But we enter another dimension— and it's just the beginning! It's the first step toward something else!

I think that the idea of "realization," even the idea of "illumination," is quite wrong. I think it's quite wrong.

I feel that each second we are PLACED before the "further" step we are supposed to take.

To me it's an absurdity; only the mind can say, "I've found the truth."

But what does the body say?

At each second, it needs to breathe. And the second before no longer counts, is no longer enough. If it stopped at the second before, it would choke to death. It needs to breathe at each second. And each second is new.

The breath of the minute before is irrelevant for tomorrow or for 30 seconds from now.

The Truth is something that is NEVER identical to itself. It's something that . . . grows with itself. It's a Movement; it isn't something static. It's a Flow.

Where is the ultimate end to that?

From the very first second when that atom exploded in the universe, everything has been in constant motion. While, on the contrary, human beings are constantly trying to stop things, to freeze them and define them. While there is constant Movement.

Mother was CONSTANTLY in motion!

"I am going as fast as a jet plane!" She used to say. And when she was told what she had said yesterday or the day before, she would say, "Oh, that's old!" And she said, "Sri Aurobindo contradicted himself a great many times, so why shouldn't we contradict ourselves!"

It's the game of the mind to want to create a philosophy once and for all, couched in neat little paragraphs.

It doesn't work that way.

One walks, one discovers. Things grow. And above all . . . I don't know, the farther one goes, the more one NEEDS something else—something truer or more genuine or . . .

It's ALWAYS different.

TOWARNICKI: *Chance, or destiny, made you choose the land of India to have that experience. Do you think it would not be possible along the Western line of thinking?*

Not only is it possible along the Western "line of thinking," but it's possible along Western STREETS, on the Western SUBWAY—it's possible at every Western second!

India . . . It so happened that Mother was here, so she . . . "caught" me, as it were—she really caught me by the scruff of the neck and pulled me out. She helped speed up my march. It happened in India, but it could have been anywhere else. It so happened that Sri Aurobindo was in India. But this has so little to do, actually, with India as a country.

It's the Earth, really.

It's the Destiny of the Earth.

It may take place more particularly in India because, after all, a certain Light has tried to incarnate in India. So it may be right that this pole is a little privileged. It's possible. But it's only a detail—it's a setting that doesn't have any definitive importance.

TOWARNICKI: *There is no exclusiveness.*

Certainly not! As I told you the other day, evolution is not Hindu.

The fact that matters is the fact of humans beings ASPIRING. Of people aspiring. They can be yellow, blue, green, Westerners, Chinese. What does it matter!

The main thing . . . the one thing is to have a NEED.

The Role of Women

TOWARNICKI: *Mother seems to have been one of the first women in the world to play that role. Generally, one finds men, gurus—*

Yes.

TOWARNICKI: —*initiates, or so-called initiates. Did Mother see a specific role for women?*

Oh, absolutely!
First of all, the woman is the base.
The woman is truly the realizer. "Realizer" means that she brings things into matter. A woman is someone who applies her consciousness to matter.
A man readily goes off into his dreams, his philosophies, his . . . all his stuff. But if he doesn't have a woman by his side to PULL him down, to help him INCARNATE his ideal, he remains stuck in his dreams.
The woman is the base.

TOWARNICKI: *(To Sujata:) What is your first name?*

SUJATA: Sujata.

TOWARNICKI: *It's Su-dja-ta?*

Yes.

TOWARNICKI: *All right. Sujata, you've been Satprem's companion for a long time. You follow the same path as he does. You often met Mother. What do you think, actually, of the particular role of woman in this kind of endeavor? And what are, for the man, the various models of woman in Indian tradition?*

(Sujata laughs)

TOWARNICKI: *Not a good question?*

151

No, your question is very good! But I was about to interrupt you to quote what Sri Aurobindo had said about Mother. *(To Satprem:)* Do you remember? Sri Aurobindo said to his disciples that had Mother not been there, his realization would have remained (how shall I put it?) on a nonmaterial plane. Mother is the one who made it possible to exist on the physical plane.

TOWARNICKI: *Did she speak of the special role of woman?*

Sri Aurobindo spoke of Mother. That's one thing. But as for women in general, well, what can I say? I don't know.

TOWARNICKI: *What about the story of the root-woman and the vine-woman?*

(Laughing) Yes.

TOWARNICKI: *That's what I wanted you to explain. In fact, how did you come across that story?*

Well, one day I was reading our Bengali poet, whom you all know, Rabindranath [Tagore]. And he said (I don't remember to whom) that he had met many women in his life, and he had found that there were two types of women: the vine-women and the root-women.

The vine-women are also very beautiful, you know! There's nothing wrong with that. But they don't help a man to settle down. Quite the contrary, they drain the man of whatever he might become or be in the truth of his being, in his depths or breadth.

Whereas the root-women remain very close to a man, which enables the man to grow toward the sun, toward the light, as it were, as a tree extends its branches.

I am just quoting from memory. *(Laughing)* That's it.

TOWARNICKI: *And what did Mother say about the special role of woman?*

Well, yes, he [Satprem] can tell you.

SATPREM: The woman is the one who has courage, far more than the man. Especially when it comes to this yoga of the body in which a man tends to regard all this as unimportant trifles—all the body's tiny suggestions that one has to battle constantly. . . .

Only a woman has the patience, really, and the courage to deal with matter in its minutest details, to seek perfection in all of matter's details.

The man just wants to soar and make a synthesis.

The woman pursues each and every thing meticulously, and each thing must be just so, proper and in its place. A woman puts things in their place.

TOWARNICKI: *A very humble task!*

Yes. But there is nothing humbler than the yoga in matter!

What is one up against, actually? A whole swarm of sordid things, constantly stirring in the consciousness.

And then, there is a sort of "health" deep down in the woman, something extremely "healthy" in a woman's very body. She is much stronger in struggling against all the morbid suggestions of decay: suggestions of illness, suggestions of death, suggestions . . .—all the suggestions one encounters when doing this yoga in matter.

She is much more healthy. Perhaps, in fact, because she has a creative role. I have never understood a realization to be complete unless a man has beside him what is called a *Shakti* in India, in other words, a REAL woman.

Things can get mired in the sentiments or even lower, in sexual relations—those are sidetracks. But there is the essence of woman, which has nothing to do with sentiments or sex. It's something of another . . . dimension.

The root of life is feminine, you know.

The creative energy is feminine.

And that's her role beside the man.

And as much as she can help him, she can also destroy him. It's obvious.

If she isn't creative, that is, if she doesn't strive toward the Light, she destroys the man.

TOWARNICKI: *And if the man doesn't strive toward the Light?*

She sinks him. . . . They both sink.

TOWARNICKI: *(To Sujata:) This is what you omitted to say a while ago.*

SUJATA: No, I don't quite agree with you. Because I feel that the woman has the CAPACITY to pull the man—even when he's sinking.

TOWARNICKI: *But can't she sink him?*

Of course, she can sink him!

She can sink him; that's what he just said. She can either sink him or help him. But I see the woman as capable—when the man is already under—she's also capable of pulling him out.

SATPREM: That's true.

Memories of Mother and Sri Aurobindo

TOWARNICKI: *(To Sujata:) You lived in the ashram from the age of twelve, didn't you?*

SUJATA: Yes . . . from the age of nine, actually.

TOWARNICKI: *And how long did you know the Mother?*

Until the end.

TOWARNICKI: *Until the end?*

Yes, for almost forty years of my life.

TOWARNICKI: *It's through a woman's eyes that you saw Mother, then?*

Oh, no! I saw Mother through a child's eyes. *(Laughing)* Absolutely. Until the end, I remained her child.

TOWARNICKI: *And how did she appear to you?*

Mother . . . Well, I'll tell you.
Traditionally it is said that the universal Mother escapes all knowledge. She has a TERRIBLE power, you know. But

for me, all that had taken the form of a mother, you understand?

(short silence)

TOWARNICKI: *Do you recall some of her words or something that particularly struck you during your life in the ashram?*

It's so difficult, you know, because my entire life was centered on her. I was trying to become rather than remember.

TOWARNICKI: *Did you have the feeling of a great Force?*

There was mainly a softness, a Love, and ESPECIALLY a comprehension. I never needed to go to her and say, "Mother, Mother, I need this or that." She understood, and acted accordingly. And even what I felt in my heart, in my feelings—I didn't need to tell Mother anything. She felt it. She understood. It's someone who "understood." It's really a blessing, you know, to have someone who understands you.

TOWARNICKI: *And what about Mother's own evolution, that gradual experience—*

Yes.

TOWARNICKI: *—she was beginning to undergo, which puzzled or even dismayed the people in the ashram? Did you sense she was doing something extraordinary?*

She mainly talked about it to Satprem. I was there, you see, because she felt that my presence didn't interfere. But it was mainly an exchange between Mother and Satprem. He followed what she said. Sometimes I understood, sometimes I didn't, but I never suspected that the people of the ashram weren't like us, loving Mother.

With their mouth, they said that they loved Mother, that they were her disciples . . . *(Laughing)* I don't know what to say. It's only AFTERWARD we found out that these were only words in their mouth, but not the real inner truth.

TOWARNICKI: *Yes, I understand. And what about your life? How did you come to the ashram? First, which part of India do you come from?*

We come from Bengal. And when we were young, my father took us to Rabindranath, at Shantiniketan. That's where we were raised, in nature.

SATPREM: Rabindranath Tagore.

SUJATA: Rabindranath Tagore, yes! *(Laughter)*
And then my mother passed away. My father loved her, truly loved her—and nothing held him anymore. So he left in search of something, and he arrived in Pondicherry, where Sri Aurobindo was.

There he found what he was looking for.

Then he brought us, his children, to Sri Aurobindo and Mother so we could see them—and above all for THEM to look at us.

TOWARNICKI: *And therefore you were able to hear the conferences or talks of Sri Aurobindo in his own language?*

No! One didn't hear Sri Aurobindo. One saw him three times a year: on his birthday, on Mother's birthday, and on the day he had what he called the "overmind realization"—have you heard of Sri Krishna? He came down and merged into Sri Aurobindo. In other words, an Avatar of the past, with all his accomplishments and realizations, immersed himself . . .

TOWARNICKI: *Incarnated?*

. . . merged.

SATPREM: Not incarnated—merged.

SUJATA: Yes, merged with Sri Aurobindo.

Those were the three days when one could see Sri Aurobindo.

Sri Aurobindo and Mother would be sitting in a little room, on a settee, and we passed before them, doing what we call *Pranam*: we placed our forehead on their feet. Because, in India, whenever we meet an elder, we usually place our forehead on his feet. It's an Indian custom.

So Mother was sitting with her feet together, and Sri Aurobindo with his legs stretched out—each one at one end of the settee, with a little space in between.

And we did our *Pranam*, as I just told you. And, oh, Sri Aurobindo's feet! . . . One literally sank into them . . . physically! It felt so soft! Those feet were so soft! I have never touched such soft feet in my life! *(laughter)* It's true! I was just a kid, you know—nine years old. But it was so difficult to stand up again! And then, we placed our head on the seat between the two of them, and they both would put their hand on the head.

SATPREM: On *your* head.

SUJATA: On my head.

TOWARNICKI: *It was a sort of blessing?*

A blessing, yes, exactly. They would bless you together. That was marvelous!
But soon it stopped because Sri Aurobindo hurt his leg, as you know.
Afterwards we no longer had the privilege of touching him. There was a sort of barrier. We filed past them in another room, in fact—we no longer went into that little room.

TOWARNICKI: *So you, too, saw Sri Aurobindo's gaze next to Mother's gaze?*

Oh, yes! But for me Mother's gaze wasn't as he described it, as Satprem described it.
There was mainly softness, you know.
For me, it was . . . it was the Mother.
It was "my" mother, in other words!
A mother doesn't look at her children with power! She looks at them with softness.
(Laughing) Actually, that reminds me of a story.
One day . . . you know, we have a season for *Puja*, when we invoke the divinities—Durga, Kali, Lakshmi, and all the goddesses—and we worship them.

Well, at a certain period in the ashram, on those days, Mother would come downstairs to meet people, and she would give her blessings to everybody.

One of those days, just before the celebration of Kali, I was working in a room, not far from where Mother was, making God knows what, maybe face powder for the ashramites . . . *(laughter)*. It was my job.

And in comes Mother. She stops in front of me and says, "Well, I am going downstairs. It's Kali's day." And she started to . . .

TOWARNICKI: *But who is Kali?*

(Laughing) Kali is the terrible Mother, who wears the heads of human beings and demons around her neck—the heads that she herself has severed. She is completely black, her hair disheveled, and she has Shiva under her feet, if you can imagine!

SATPREM: Shiva is the—

SUJATA: He's the supreme God. So she has the supreme God at her feet, if you can picture that! *(Laughing)* Okay. So she's really terrible, that Kali.

So Mother says to me, "Oh, you know, today is Kali's day. Do you know Kali?" I look at Mother without a word, with a slight smile. And Mother starts taking on Kali's appearance—that terrible appearance, you know. A Power that anybody who . . . (you know Ramakrishna, who worshipped Kali?), well, anybody would have been crushed by that Force, that Power.

But, I don't know, I am Mother's child, so I just stood there, looking at her. After some time, Mother says, "My, you don't flinch. Aren't you afraid?" And I replied, "Little Mother, you're my mother! So you can be anything, take on any appearance, I am your child! You're my mother!" *(Laughing)* Mother herself was astounded by my answer.

Indeed, for me she was always a mother.

TOWARNICKI: *How old were you then?*

At the time . . . I was sixteen, seventeen at the most.

Sujata: Mother's Agenda

TOWARNICKI: *All right. So you stayed in the ashram until Mother's passing.*

SUJATA: Yes.

TOWARNICKI: *What happened after she passed away ?*

(short silence)

Well, we lived a little away. . . . Someone came and told us that Mother . . . They had taken Mother's body downstairs—removed her from her room and taken her downstairs—and people were filing past.

We had never believed that Mother would leave her body.

In any case, we went to see. Satprem and I went and watched (Satprem must have told you how it was[1]). . . .

I am skipping a lot of things, you understand.

---

1. Satprem had not told anything, actually. Six and a half hours after Mother's heart had stopped, the disciples took her from her living quarters and placed her in a hall, beneath a metal ceiling and scorching reflectors, while thousands of people started to file past her—and she had said, "This body must be left in peace."

161

Later . . . there was that document of Mother's, which she called her *Agenda*. That is, all the conversations she had had for years and years and years with Satprem.

People wanted to have them published immediately in "fragments" —in small fragments. But Satprem remembered what Mother had said: "One day we will publish it as a whole—integrally." So that's what we tried to do. And from one day to the next, the ashram officials (the new officials, that is) started to show what they had in mind.

First, they decided to "edit" the *Agenda*. They wanted to censor Mother's words.

It was really astonishing, because how could they possibly know how to connect what Mother had said to Satprem in 1958, and then in 1968? Only Satprem knew what had happened. Only he knew how to make connections in all that material.

But they were adamant. They said, "No. Only the senior sadhaks (as they called them) know what should be done."

And so we began to think that "something isn't right here."

So we tried to publish it integrally. We put a note in an ashram journal announcing the publication of the *Agenda*. But later we had to remove that note because the ashram trustees didn't want it.

So what to do?

Then gradually we began to see their real face.

But because Satprem had written his trilogy on Mother, after Mother's passing, he was asked to go to France. And there we learned that Satprem had the right to publish Mother's words since he was the one Mother had talked to! Until then, we didn't know that. It's only in France that we learned it.

And that's how we began publishing Mother's conversations with Satprem, what is known as *Mother's Agenda*.

TOWARNICKI: *Which covers what period?*

It began in 1957—even before, in 1956.
Although at that time, there was no tape recorder. . . .

SATPREM: At that time, I kept running away from the ashram!

SUJATA: Not only that, but there was no tape recorder.

TOWARNICKI: *So what is the period covered?*

From 1955 until 1973.

Auroville: The Assassination Attempt

TOWARNICKI: *Satprem, what is your connection with the project of Auroville, its construction, its life?*

SATPREM: Oh, Mother told me many things about Auroville!
But to tell the truth, in the beginning, I wasn't in the least interested in Auroville. What interested me was Mother's experience.
But, of course, Auroville was the attempt to incarnate that experience on a human scale and, above all, collectively.
Can that new Force, as it were, incarnate itself? Can that new species actually grow and develop in a group of human beings living together, in a collective environment?
That's what the attempt of Auroville was all about.
But I didn't actually get involved with it, because it wasn't at all my concern. My concern was Mother's experience.
I began to involve myself in it . . . after Mother's departure.
Indeed, what was left after Mother's departure?
What, practically and concretely, was left?

163

Three things were left.

First, that fabulous *Agenda*, those conversations about Mother's experience—I was with her for nineteen years—all the conversations where she explains the course she followed. It's a fabulous document.

That's what was left, first—that *Agenda*.

Then there was Auroville, which was the attempt to IN-CARNATE that experience.

TOWARNICKI: *What actually is Auroville?*

Auroville is in the canyons near Pondicherry. It's a plot of red soil—there's really nothing: a few huts and a group of people from just about every country in the world seeking "something else," without quite knowing what that "something else" is, but who NEED . . . well, another type of life than the one we live, painfully, a little everywhere on earth. And who have more or less understood that Mother and Sri Aurobindo were trying to make something different emerge in this human matter.

The third thing that Mother left was the ashram.

And the ashram . . . meant, well, people entrenched in the truth. They were the "owners"—they owned Mother and Sri Aurobindo. They were the heirs.

And of course, they knew everything. They had nothing to learn from anybody. They did their meditations, they did their . . .—they were the owners.

Whereas Auroville was another story altogether! This was a group of slightly eccentric people, apparently, who didn't much care for meditation and all that, but who wanted to LIVE a more real life, a more LIVING life, and were ready to try the experiment.

So, naturally, the static forces, those that didn't want to budge—who were entrenched in the truth—immediately tried to claim ownership over BOTH *Mother's Agenda* AND Auroville.

And when they tried to assert their ownership over the *Agenda*, meaning, to censor it—because they were very frightened of what Mother might have said—I refused.

SUJATA: He just couldn't.

SATPREM: It was really impossible, you know, for me to agree to censor Mother.

And what did those people understand anyway?

Mother kept telling me . . . how many times did she say, "They don't understand anything!"

And so those people who didn't understand anything wanted the "senior disciples" to evaluate which of Mother's words were "valid."

What did they understand of what was "valid" in Mother?

And what a pretension to think: this is valid and that is not.

They even went so far as to say that the *Agenda* was not authentic! Because it had not been reviewed and edited by the ashram officials. But that's past history. Past history, well, anyway . . . I fought a lot.

And in the same way, they tried to take possession of Auroville.

There were a lot of foreigners in Auroville—many people of almost every nationality. And India had been one of the countries to help raise the funds for building Auroville—you need a lot of money to get something so huge started. The man who, during Mother's time, had raised the funds—tried to raise the funds—declared himself the "owner of Auroville."

And since he was a very clever businessman, he tried to cash in on "The Great Spiritual Enterprise"—a big Auroville-Disney Land, with friends in America, Germany, France, Italy, and everywhere. But the Aurovilians refused to play his game.

And that's when I came into the picture. Because I SAW what a fraud it was, you see. So I tried to warn the Aurovilians against it, because at the beginning they weren't even aware of the danger.

It wasn't another Disney Land that we wanted to make in Auroville.

It wasn't a spiritual circus for the benefit of television networks, you see. It was something . . . it was a difficult endeavor.

So, first, the Aurovilians had to understand that.

But then those Auroville owners, well, used every possible means to . . . Yes, that's about all one can say.

TOWARNICKI: *You are not directly accusing anybody here, but perhaps we could talk about the attacks . . .*

But accusing is . . .

TOWARNICKI: *. . . And in particular, if you agree, I would like the story of the canyons. Why not tell it?*

Well, yes, someone tried to kill me—that's true. But it's very difficult to say who.

TOWARNICKI: *What happened?*

Every day I take a walk in the canyons—I used to take a walk in the canyons—near Pondicherry. Then I sat on the

166

edge of the canyons and I looked out . . . into the distance. There were sea gulls flying all the way back into the canyons. I liked . . . I liked it. It cleansed me of everything. And one day, as I was sitting as usual, three men came up to me—they came out of a depression in the ground where they were hidden, straight at me—and I immediately knew and felt: "They are coming to kill me."

Then I don't know what happened (I really had nothing to do with it), but I was as if annulled: there was not a single reaction in me. I looked at those men, and nothing stirred in me. There was not a single emotion, not a single vibration. All of a sudden, it's as if I had been PHYSICALLY emptied of all human reaction. I looked at all that the way one looks at something happening to somebody else.

Two of the men came in front of me while the third one, the killer, remained behind (I had noticed him immediately; he had big golden eyes). And I just sat there. They started to talk between themselves (the two in front of me), making a gesture of tossing me into the canyon. I listened to them, and I was as if transparent—as if it all went through me without . . . without causing any reaction.

At one point, something in me said, "Now stand up." So I stood up. I had my back to the canyon. Now, all three men were in front of me. Two took me by the hands, one on each side. One of them removed my watch, maybe to make it appear as a theft, I don't know. Then the killer got in front of me.

And then . . . I don't know, his fist was down, and he began to raise his fist, you know, to push me. I followed the motion of that fist, and our eyes met. . . . The whole thing was in a sort of . . . I can't say, it was so transparent, as if nothing were happening. Then . . . I saw his fist coming back down, dropping. He looked as if he were a little lost. And all at once, they turned on their heels and fled, as if in a panic.

And suddenly I realized what had just happened and my heart started pounding! I suddenly realized that something had happened. But the whole time they were there, I was as if . . . it's as if absolutely nothing were happening!

I think I understood (afterward) what had physically happened. . . . In fact, this is the "other state," the other state of pure cellular matter, free of its coverings—that ever-present layer of the physical mind with its anxieties, its fears, its . . . habit of reacting—all that covers us, that covers our body and our existence, that attracts death, attracts every accident. For we constantly live in fear of this or that, or with a question about this or that. . . . Well, during the five, six or seven minutes that episode lasted, I was completely null. In other words, there was NOT A SINGLE VIBRATION in my body. My heart was not beating faster than usual. I was looking at all that as if it didn't have any reality. Hence it's as if their force, I guess, went through me without encountering any resistance or obstacle. They couldn't latch onto anything. Whereas if there had been the slightest reaction of fear in me, some apprehension or even a movement of SELF-DEFENSE, they would have killed me instantly! But it all went through me completely unobstructed. I was like thin air. You can't assassinate thin air!

TOWARNICKI: *There was nothing left?*

Nothing left! I was truly NULL. It was . . . quite extraordinary, I must say.

It's only afterward, when they suddenly started to flee in a panic, that I MYSELF became aware of myself again. And my heart started pounding: "Oh, somebody just tried to kill you!"

I said to myself, "Oh, somebody tried to kill you!"

But the whole time it lasted, there was absolutely nothing! And if I had felt something, there WOULD have been something!

The Man After Man: The Next State

I think this is . . . (what shall I say?) the "perception" of the next state in matter. It's a state where things no longer have any reality—where death, accidents, illness, attacks, this thing and that no longer have any reality! For pure, simple, childlike matter—as it is—all that doesn't have any reality!

We know how children go unscathed through all sorts of incredible things, because, for them, those things don't have any reality! Their matter is not yet too "covered up" by all the habits we stick on it.

Thus, one can have a sense of what the next state in matter might be: a matter that has lost its fear, its apprehensions, its habits, its accidents, its death—all the things that have hung over it for thousands of years.

And what is pure matter like?

It is childlike: there are no more accidents, no more laws. . . . It falls, and doesn't hurt itself.

TOWARNICKI: *Is this what "the man after man" will be, do you think?*

It is just a GLIMPSE of what the man after man can be—just a glimpse. And I think that some people can have that type of experience in which suddenly the "weight" is off us and our reactions. And no accident is possible! Bullets can be fired, but they don't touch us!

TOWARNICKI: *And what about the state of "supra-consciousness" mentioned by Sri Aurobindo?*

He says "supra-mental."

Precisely, it's a state outside of the mind. We are . . . a tissue of mental reactions—of a very rudimentary nature, but we are nonetheless completely covered by the mind. Our slightest reaction is observed . . . leaves its imprint, its memory.

So a supramental state is a state free of those imprints, free of those memories.

And then we're free!

Matter is in fact free! There's nothing more plastic and supple in the world than matter. It is capable of everything. It can adapt to everything, take every shape. But first, we must obviously get out of the conditioning. We must break through all those mental layers covering up our natural state: the pure cell, without fear, without limits. For matter also communicates with everything, you see. Matter is not confined in a particular body; it instantaneously communicates with everything. Because it IS everywhere. A physicist will tell you the same thing: "You can't cut up matter into small pieces." What is felt here is instantaneously felt there. It's THE SAME thing. One and the SAME being, one and the SAME Vibration, or one and the SAME wavelength. So, obviously, it knows itself, whether it's here or ten thousand miles away!

It's therefore a completely different MODE of life that is emerging.

That's what the man after man is: no more separation, no more barriers, no more incomprehension. Something begins to be light and . . . natural.

TOWARNICKI: *In his own system of thought, the German philosopher Heidegger uses the German word gelassenheit, which means roughly to "let be."*

Yes.

TOWARNICKI: *A state of surrender, of openness, of availability to an answer.*

Yes, yes, yes! It's . . . exactly that.
But not just in the mind, or in the heart, or even in the sensations—it must be like that IN THE BODY.
It's a state a child knows very well. A child is totally surrendered. What should he be afraid of?
Fear begins with memory.
Limits begin with memory.
That's the beginning of the fishbowl.

TOWARNICKI: *But we use . . . we speak of "body," then we speak of "consciousness."*

But it's the same thing!
Precisely! . . . That's exactly what we realize immediately: that matter is consciousness; that consciousness is matter. If you consider Einstein's equation: Matter = Energy, one term is missing in that equation, which is that: Matter = Energy = Consciousness.

TOWARNICKI: *But then, because our vocabulary is still probably too approximate, our emphasis on the "body" may stem from the fact that in the past we have too often only emphasized the mind, or what we called "consciousness." Shouldn't we use another word, then, which would be neither "body" (which is limited) nor "consciousness" (which is also limited), in order to define or isolate that dimension where the two different realities, the two aspects merge?*

But they are not different! They are not different. They are the SAME thing.

TOWARNICKI: *In different aspects.*

It's we who see aspects. When it's uncovered, there are no "aspects"—IT IS. It's something one experiences.

The vibration of consciousness in matter is something one can perceive the way one perceives the fragrance of a flower. The consciousness of matter is like its fragrance, if you will.

You see, we are constantly SEEING matter as a "thing" or an "object." But in that pure state, you EXPERIENCE it—you experience matter. It isn't something you look at; you're in it.

SUJATA: May I say something?

It's a little like a tree, you know. It's the same energy in the tree that makes the leaves, the flowers, and the fruit. For us, they are different aspects, apparently, yet it's the same thing!

SATPREM: Yes, exactly. It's one and the same Energy.

TOWARNICKI: *You must admit that, even today, it's difficult to speak of those things. As if our ordinary vocabulary were still . . .*

Our vocabulary mentalizes everything. It sees everything as an "object." It sees everything as something "different" from itself. It's a constant cinematic performance. It is never IN the thing. . . . In mental life as we know it, we are never in things. We are always in our ideas about things or in our perception of them.

While the beginning of true life—the truly human life—is something one no longer looks at; one FEELS ONESELF, EXPERIENCES ONESELF—one lives in everything. And not as something different, but as part of the same body.

It's very difficult to speak of that other life, of course. But it's clearly another life IN matter. Another mode of being IN matter.

In the canyons I had a glimpse of that transparent state . . . There one realizes that no death is possible—it simply doesn't exist. No accident is possible. No illness is possible. Those are just the "ordinary" falsehoods. We live in a deceptive habit that CREATES illnesses, accidents, death and all the rest. And just on the other side of that "membrane," well, there exists an incredible freedom—a BODILY FREEDOM!

(pause)

TOWARNICKI: *This is the real mystery: that we exist. And not in the manner of an animal, not in the manner of an inanimate object, but in a special manner. As if there were a special design in man—which doesn't take anything away from the tree, the stone or the animal—*

173

But of course, there is a design! . . .

TOWARNICKI: —*but which imparts to man a special destiny in the whole.*

Of course, he has a very special destiny! Of all the species, he's the only one capable of going beyond the law of his particular bowl.

Every species . . . The matter of a fish and the matter of a man are quite similar, as you know. There is no fundamental difference between them, except for the fact that the fish are the prisoners of a certain habit, and they are quite content in their habit. In fact, every species is quite content—except ours. Why?

Precisely because we are CAPABLE of doing what no other species can do: go down to the bottom of our bowl to see what it's made of, and BREAK the habit.

A fish can't get out of its habit of being a fish.

But a human being can get out of his habit of being a human being.

And that's exactly what the path of Mother and Sri Aurobindo is: Instead of getting out above, on an apex of the Spirit, they went down to the bottom of the bowl to see what was there. And they found that the bowl was merely the product of a certain habit, and that one could break through it and come out into another "being" or "mode of being."

And that's probably why we are being asphyxiated and our human life is so painful—to FORCE us to find the real KEY.

Other species do not need a key—they are content.

And I think that all the suffering of our time, in which everything is so stifling and seems on the verge of collapse, is evidence that we are nearing the point when we will be COLLECTIVELY able to break the fishbowl.

And emerge where?
In the human being, really.
Something we are not yet at all.

TOWARNICKI: *You mean at present?*

We are an aggregate of habits that thinks it is human, thinks it is philosophical, and this and that. But this is not really the human being.
We don't yet know the real human being.
We are just apprentice humans.

TOWARNICKI: *One can also envision the question from another angle. We talk a lot about man, of course, since he is supposed to have a special role to play in the universe. But if man gets out of the fishbowl, it might not be for his benefit alone—to create a hyper-consciousness for himself—it might be to help what is not him come into expression, existence, manifestation?*

What do you mean by "not him"?

TOWARNICKI: *Well, man was born after everything else in the universe!*

Yes.

TOWARNICKI: *So what about the rest? The focus is always on him. Why that hyper-consciousness? Why get out of the bowl? To make man a little happier? A little more serene? There is also a whole connection between himself and what is not him.*

But every relationship and exchange is different the minute you're out of the bowl! The very notion of "self" is no longer the same! I was never so free and invulnerable as when I was completely null in those canyons. There was no "me" at all in this. If there had been a "me," they would have killed me instantly. The "me" is TOTALLY mortal.

"Me" is the falsehood.

But that doesn't mean that, on the other side of the bowl, you lose all individuality! There remains that point of reference which was painstakingly built for 30, 40 or 50 years— that point of reference remains. But you no longer feel yourself as a Me (with a capital M).

TOWARNICKI: *What happens then?*

One should only speak of those things from experience. My own experience is very "slight." I can't . . .

TOWARNICKI: *Does a mountain appear different? Does water appear different? Does the sky appear different?*

Mother said many things in regard to material appearances. She said a lot of very fascinating things. But we should let her say it herself.

As for my own experience, it's mainly a radical difference in the perception of human beings—what moves them, what drives them. I feel those things in a very different way.

TOWARNICKI: *For man does not come first. Before man, there is "That" from which—*

—from which he stems?

176

TOWARNICKI: *Before man, "there is." When a man opens his eyes, there already is.*

Indeed!

TOWARNICKI: *He isn't first. He isn't the Lord and Master of the universe, as has been often said. A child barely opens his eyes (even the first child in the world), and something is given to him that he has not produced and upon which he will base himself: "there is." Perhaps this is the primary word, the original base: "there is." "That is." And man is already in the "That is."*

Yes.

TOWARNICKI: *And from then on . . .*

But the point is, we can't get out of the human—our fishbowl—unless we are in contact with the "That is"!
And "That is" is something one can BREATHE in the body, you see. It isn't an idea. There is no getting out of the human bowl without first being in contact with the "That is."

TOWARNICKI: *But the "That is" . . .*

The "That is" is everywhere and everything.
And that's why there's instant "communication" with everything, understanding of everything, HELP from everything.

TOWARNICKI: *Always and only "human understanding"! Let me formulate a paradox. What if one day things were to "understand" us better than we do?*

But things understand us very well already!

A plant understands quite well the kind of manipulation you have.

I think the whole world understands well, except us!

Actually, EVERYTHING understands well. A tree understands quite well what is there. I've touched a lot of rocks . . . I love rocks, and there is something in a rock that feels.

(short silence)

I think we've turned things completely upside down: we have assumed that man had the prerogative of consciousness and everything else was, well, slightly retarded. But it doesn't work that way!

I even think that we are the only ones not conscious.

We are conscious of "us." That's our big problem. But it's also our lever, because thanks to that falsehood, as it were, we are forced to find the key.

And the falsehood is to think of oneself as a "me"—a separate consciousness, alone capable of being conscious.

That's the falsehood.

On the other side of the fishbowl, things don't work that way. From the little I have experienced of it, there is instant "communication" with everything. A kind of understanding that has nothing to do with objects—you understand something because you're IN it.

And then there's another kind of power! It's a whole other "mode" of being altogether.

That example in the canyons is very telling: those men couldn't kill.

The Battle of the World

TOWARNICKI: *What is Sri Aurobindo's position, and perhaps Mother's, with regard to Zen?*

That I don't know. They didn't specifically say anything about it.

But, you see, EVERYTHING is good. EVERYTHING is the "guru"—the liquor store down the street, and the Zen Master, and the bird or the . . . Absolutely everything—the bus you just missed. Everything is the guru. Everything HELPS. Yet, instead of realizing that each thing is an indication and a help, we usually walk right by, looking at it with customary eyes. In other words, we see nothing.

So Zen is very good, Christianity is very good, the liquor store is very good—provided we know how to open our eyes and use what is in front of us to learn the lesson we are supposed to learn.

So nothing should be judged; nothing should be seen as high or low. Everything is a staff to help us walk on the road.

The mistake is to say: "Zen, and that's it," or Christianity. (As a matter of fact, I don't even think Zen says such a thing.) To say "that's it" about anything is the one deadly sin. We are already dead.

TOWARNICKI: *Aren't you afraid that people will accuse you of creating a sort of retreat for yourself? Of removing yourself from the world, in a way?*

Heavens! My struggle is far from being removed!

I don't know . . . All my life, I have been involved in one struggle or another. The road I followed has very little to do with retreating, I can assure you! I've faced all sorts of

179

beings, all sorts of countries and circumstances. I've lugged bags of mica, probed swamps in search of gold, dug trenches . . . faced all sorts of things. Where is the retreat?

And now, because I seem to be in the mountains . . . My life is a FIERCE battle.

To write "purely," to try to say things truthfully, with force and sincerity, is a battle. It's a battle to let it go through you "purely"—to express "purely" what has to be expressed.

TOWARNICKI: *While the rest of the world wrestles with difficulties, injustice . . .*

But that's what we are fighting for!

We are fighting, precisely, for this poor world. To try to filter a HOPE and ANOTHER POSSIBILITY into it.

TOWARNICKI: *What about the struggle on the human, social plane?*

Yes, yes, yes.

TOWARNICKI: *Do you understand it?*

But fighting is indispensable, of course!

However, the solution is not where they're seeking it.

The one indispensable thing is to fight. Whether on the right or on the left, what matters is to put all your heart into it, everything you've got and all your sincerity—whatever side you're on. That's what's important. Because it makes something ELSE grow and develop in the being.

That's the essential part.

But to believe that the solution is capitalist or Marxist, Maoist or religious or spiritual is proof that our old human stupidity is still trying to put things into a box.

That's not the solution.

The solution lies in going to the bottom of the fishbowl, in moving on to our true human breath—to what we really are.

The Failure. The Cry. The Fairy Tale

In fact, we are LED there, through that relentless pounding on all nations, all human consciousnesses, all churches, all groups. . . . One feels as if everything were being kneaded, ground to powder in order to reach the bottom of it all. We are being shown how contradictory and ineffective all our human solutions are—how they lead nowhere.

You can take the example, in India, of a man I like very much, named Mr. Tata, who did a lot to help Auroville out of the clutches of those spiritual mercenaries. Here is a man who, in human terms, was the head of fabulous industrial enterprises in India, who was the first man to make long-distance flights—who was a courageous man. Well, at the end of all those years of struggle and apparent success, he acknowledges an abysmal failure. He had hoped that his industries, his discoveries and huge organization would help lessen India's poverty—he is crushed by her misery. And he realizes, that despite all his industries and foundations, he is incapable of helping his Indian brothers. He is distressed. He ends up in failure.

And I think that EVERYTHING is ending up in failure, to open or show us the only possible door.

You can also take André Malraux as a Western representative of a certain brilliant success. But Malraux was a

181

failure—he ended up in failure. What was the practical result of all his marvelous mental juggling?

TOWARNICKI: *Did you meet him?*

I didn't meet him, but Malraux is someone I really understood in my heart. His courage, his determination to put into action what he felt—it all had a meaning for me. But he was never able (it seems he struggled and fought a lot), but he was never able to go beyond his mental jugglings—marvelous as they may be, but . . . He was marvelous inside the fishbowl, but he was never able to get to the other side.

And I have the feeling this applies to every apparently successful life. Take the great industrialist Tata or the great intellectual André Malraux, or any "great" man—I think even Einstein, at the end of his life, came up against a wall.

We are all up against a wall. Whether Marxist, Christian, Hindu or Chinese, we all end up against a wall.

So each person has to fight in his own way. If you are born Chinese, well, fight in your Chinese way. If you are born in Moscow, well, fight as a Muscovite. That's perfectly fine.

But the solution doesn't lie in any of those places.

That's what human beings have to understand. Because to understand . . . is to call.

If the fish (to use the same metaphor) had not begun to asphyxiate, it would never have taken the necessary "step" to mutate—to become amphibian.

The world needs a certain degree of asphyxiation, and all of a sudden there's a cry—a CRY.

Then everything becomes possible.

Then this fishbowl, which seems so formidable, becomes paper-thin, without any reality. It can suddenly burst, or melt away.

But there has to be a CRY. There has to be a CALL.

TOWARNICKI: *And to conclude, if you could speak to children . . .*

But this is a fairy tale! Mother said.
On the other side of this formidable, awesome, electronic, implacable and biological bowl, a fairy tale awaits us!
And one can see it's a fairy tale, because there are no more "laws." All the laws were in our MIND.
On the other side, another kind of lightness begins to exist. It's a . . . humanity that's inconceivable, except for children, in fact.

TOWARNICKI: *What would you tell them?*

To a child?
I am not sure you would need to tell much to a child, because he would experience it spontaneously. He would merge with the wave, lose himself with the sea gull. . . . A child—one who isn't spoiled—LIVES that naturally.

(short silence)

A child may be a case where the least said the better, except for stories and fairy tales.
And we spend our time covering up that powerful simplicity of the child with all sorts of "You can't do this," "That isn't possible," "It doesn't work that way." We put layer upon layer of prohibitions and impossibilities. Then it's hopeless.
That's what is being broken—all our layers of impossibility.

183

What Is Not Twenty Centimes?

The Technical Civilization: A Child Will Destroy it

TOWARNICKI: *Satprem, today the world of science and technology is firmly established, rooted in the world, from east to west and north to south. It's a formidable force. How can it . . .*

SATPREM: Oh, a grain of sand—just a grain of sand and the whole machine shuts down. Absolutely. Sorry, I interrupted you.

TOWARNICKI: *. . . How can a spiritual experience conceivably shake, dismantle, transform this gigantic apparatus?*

(short silence)

It's an enormous monster, but . . . it's a fragile one.

As early as 1910 or 12 Sri Aurobindo had looked at that Western civilization, and he had had those rather terrible words. I remember, he had said this (in one of his aphorisms):

"Europe prides herself on her practical and scientific organisation and efficiency. I am waiting till her organisation is perfect; then a child shall destroy her."[1]

He had seen that.

All it takes is a grain of sand in that enormous machine.

We saw it in 1973, suddenly: Just turn off the oil spigot, and everything starts coming apart.

That enormous machine is a bit like our spacecraft. We are, in fact, in a sort of enormous scientific "capsule," and all it takes is one little loose nut for the whole capsule to become deadly.

All it takes is a little loose nut, and everything stops.

How do we know that the events of 1973—the first oil embargo—will not happen again on a more radical scale? Or even something quite unexpected, which nobody had thought of—and suddenly that enormous machine comes to a halt.

Look, the moment that machine can no longer be fed, it'll spread from Lubbock, Texas, to Hong Kong and Washington—everything will stop.

And man will suddenly find himself without his machinery . . . exactly as he was five thousand years ago!

And this is truly when, if such a breakdown occurs, man will open his eyes to a . . . rather frightening realization about himself and his condition. He will abruptly find himself as if at the beginning of civilization, but with the inner consciousness of the entire cycle he has undergone. And he will say to himself, "What . . . what is it?"

---

1. *Thoughts and Aphorisms.*

What will he feel he has accomplished?

That's when, perhaps, he will come to that "pure" moment, deep inside, when a man has to BE something. Not just a sum of machines + a family + philosophy + religion, but truly his own REAL human heartbeat.

If one such second seizes hold of humanity because its machinery breaks down, then, truly, another dimension will be able to take over the human heart.

After Marx and Mao, What?

TOWARNICKI: *One meets many distinguished people and scholars, in India as well as in the West, who are troubled by India's condition, the problem of over-population. Do you think it is a serious problem?*

Oh, certainly!

TOWARNICKI: *Talking about overpopulation, J.R.D. Tata made the comment that between 1946 and 1967 three hundred million people were added to the population of India.*

Yes.

TOWARNICKI: *And between 1980 and 2000 or 2025, it seems inevitable that India's population will increase by another three hundred million people.*

Yes. It's an insoluble problem. Insoluble, because NOBODY in India has the courage to do what is necessary. Indira Gandhi tried, two or three years ago, to control the population. But her efforts were shamelessly distorted, with charges

187

that she was sterilizing women, sterilizing men—a whole political propaganda campaign was mounted against her effort to fight the REAL danger threatening India. And she was so thoroughly burned that I doubt she'll have the courage to try again.

And yet, this is the central problem of India. There are no others. That's the only problem. But NOBODY wants to see it. NOBODY.

So it's insoluble.

Which means that one day, as usual, Nature will probably say, "Enough is enough." She will make a little earthquake or something of the kind and set this swarming mass straight once and for all. But there's no doubt that something HAS to happen to stop this tide.

And not just in India, of course. Take China: one billion people.

TOWARNICKI: *What are the obstacles? On the one hand, according to J.R.D. Tata, the pioneer of Indian industry, the socialist (or pseudo-socialist) kind of economic policy in India since Nehru leads to an enormous bureaucracy, a huge administration. . . .*

Yes, an octopus!

TOWARNICKI: *Now he has a sort of apprehension, or fear, which is twofold: first, the appalling tide of overpopulation. He says that any attempt to help the situation is immediately swallowed up—*

Yes, he's right.

TOWARNICKI: *—by it.*

He's absolutely right.

TOWARNICKI: *It's endless.*

Yes.

TOWARNICKI: *And secondly, he seems to fear that the world situation—as well as future crises awaiting us—will force the Soviet Union to make a strategic move and seize Europe's industrial riches, among other things. Not because the Soviet Union is evil, but because, as I mentioned earlier, for a good chess player Europe is a square up for grabs, and it would help neutralize the United States.*

I don't believe so.
If they launched a war in Europe, where would the "industrial riches" be? The square would be empty.
That's where I disagree with him.

TOWARNICKI: *Well. Perhaps because you are farther from—*

It doesn't work that way.
That's what Mother saw. That's what Sri Aurobindo had seen. And what they saw was behind the immediate appearances—the forces that drive nations. It isn't a question of millions of dollars or tanks or . . . Things don't work that way. There are forces in the background. And that's what Mother and Sri Aurobindo saw.

TOWARNICKI: *Yes.*

And they saw the danger with China.
And I also feel that danger.

TOWARNICKI: *You also feel it.*

Oh, yes!

The Soviet Union has come to the END of its communist experience. As Mother said, "They've come to the end of their experience and they don't know how to get out of it." They are ready for something else.[1]

So, instead of pushing them to the wall, of forcing them to resort to desperate acts; instead of surrounding them like a pack of wolves—everybody is constantly saying, "The Soviet Union, the Soviet Union," crying wolf, you know, while the Chinese are doing their level best to . . . (how shall I put it?) stir up that anti-Soviet sentiment—because if the Soviets feel encircled, surrounded on all sides, they can be pushed into desperate acts. When, in fact, all they want is to find a way out of their communist impasse.

They've come to the end of their road.

TOWARNICKI: *Well, of course, it's a very debatable issue.*

But what I say is, inwardly, they've come to the end of their road.

The real question, however, is, after Marx and Mao, what? Well, Sri Aurobindo has a certain answer to that. And an answer in matter. A true materialism. Perhaps a "divine materialism"?

---

1. These words (spoken in 1980) find a striking echo today (1989) in "perestroika" and Mikhail Gorbachev's attempt to reshape Soviet society, while the world discovers with horror a forgotten face of China in Tiananmen Square. (translator's note)

J.R.D. Tata and Auroville, Changing Human Nature

TOWARNICKI: *And how do you explain J.R.D. Tata's helping Auroville?*

Ah, that is something else.

TOWARNICKI: *Can one talk about it?*

Of course, one can.

TOWARNICKI: *Do you know exactly what he did?*

He helped Auroville a great deal.
Auroville was besieged by a corrupt police, paid by the "owners of Auroville" (in quotation marks).

TOWARNICKI: *The owners of the land?*

Yes. . . .
They weren't the "owners." Mother had put a few people in charge (you've got to have funds to start building a city); she had asked one or two of her disciples to concentrate particularly on raising funds wherever they could to help in the birth or creation of Auroville.

And the people she had entrusted with raising funds to help in the development of Auroville are the very ones who declared themselves the "owners of Auroville"! It's quite simple and straightforward: "Mother is gone, so we are the owners."

And so those "owners" (who were unscrupulous people—really crooks, in fact) used every means in the book to try to keep their authority over Auroville. And unfortunately, with corruption pervading everything in India, they paid EVERY-BODY—the police, the villagers, various officials—in order to have the government expel, or to choke the lifeline of, those residents of Auroville who refused to participate in the swindle and the big spiritual business. They used absolutely everything. They had some of them put in jail, they . . . Oh, there were all sorts of awful things!

TOWARNICKI: *Including aggression?*

Yes, absolutely, including aggression!

This is where Mr. Tata was very helpful. . . . You see, in fact, Auroville needed to be protected against those mercenaries. And he agreed to—

TOWARNICKI: *That's really something . . .*

He agreed that his name be used, and he said, "I guarantee Auroville's integrity." Well, the moment somebody like Mr. Tata guarantees something, it puts an end to a lot of intrigues; it kept a lot of little hyenas from perpetrating their mischief.

He was very helpful in that way.

And not only did he give his personal guarantee, but several of us joined together to found . . . not an institute, but a sort of society, called *Auromitra*, meaning "The Friends of Auroville," to protect Auroville from these crooks.

TOWARNICKI: *And why did he do it?*

Out of love, of course! Simply because he believed; he believed in those young people. . . . The group of a few hundred young people living there: Germans, Italians, Canadians, Americans, French. He had seen them. He had seen their vitality and sincerity. And even if it looked eccentric or uncustomary, there was something healthy about it, something genuine, authentic.

He had seen that.

So he said to himself, "I am going to guarantee the integrity of these people."

And he had seen, on the other side, the people who called themselves "the owners"—he clearly saw that they were crooks.

So, in his way, as the generous and very simple man that he is (he is indeed a very simple and straightforward man; Tata is a man who has a heart, a big heart), he said to himself, "I am going to protect these young people from the intrigues and corruption of those people"—who brought false charges against them to the police, who had them arrested . . .

He gave his personal guarantee. He had the guts to say, "No, no, no, this is not how things are."

TOWARNICKI: *You have seen J.R.D. Tata several times, haven't you?*

Yes.

TOWARNICKI: *Have you talked to him?*

Yes.

TOWARNICKI: *He knows what you have tried to do, what Mother has done. He even went there. . . .*

Yes.

Yes, but he doesn't really understand how Mother's and Sri Aurobindo's undertaking can help present humanity in a practical and concrete way. He doesn't understand that.

Because, for him, the problem is mainly an economic one.

Yet, as he himself admits, what is needed is a change in human nature.

In truth, it is not so much a change in India's pocketbook that is needed as a change in human nature. If you don't change human nature, you always end up with failure.

In other words, it is not an economic problem.

TOWARNICKI: *Or perhaps it's both. He thinks that, short of an economic solution, all attempts to ameliorate human nature—the "quality of mankind," as the founder of the Club of Rome put it—are bound to fail, because they will be thwarted by other forces we failed to take into account. If we let the fire in a nearby forest go unchecked, without fighting it, what is the sense of an experience aimed at opening the way to a future species? Will the force of such an experience be able to control the fire? Or will the fire inexorably and inevitably spread and end up destroying . . .*

What you are saying is very true, but we keep talking of the future species as if . . . as if it were a thing of the future! But we are RIGHT IN IT—the process is taking place now.

We clothe the phenomenon in wrong explanations. But the real phenomenon is of an evolutionary order.

TOWARNICKI: *Exactly.*

The truth is, the old species is being broken apart so another possibility can emerge from it.
And that's the real key to everything.

TOWARNICKI: *So . . .*

The new species isn't in the next decade; it's right here and now.
We are living it. We are in the process of living it.

Instinct

TOWARNICKI: *Does that plunge or descent into the cellular consciousness have anything to do with what we call instinct.*

Instinct?
What do we mean by instinct?
These are mental categorizations. It's like sticking a label on something to avoid looking at the contents.
What is instinct?
The instinct of a human being? The instinct of a bird?
The instinct of what? The instinct of the rock?
Well, the instinct of the world is . . . is TO BE THE WORLD!
The instinct of the nucleus is to snap up electrons!
The instinct of the bird is to communicate with everything it needs, without any separation!
What we don't see is that the world is a single unity, without any separation. We think that we can only perceive the world through a certain instinct we have of it. But it doesn't work that way! Does Mr. Towarnicki have the "instinct" of his big toe or is his big toe part of him?

TOWARNICKI: *Can man derive something, learn something, by watching animals, insects?*

Well, he can certainly learn what he has forgotten.

You see, everything communicates in this world; there are no separations. We are the ones who are completely separated from the world.

For a bird, a lobster, a beaver the world is immediate! They communicate with everything they need.

Why do they communicate?

Certainly NOT because they "look" at something far away and strive to see it better and . . . They instantaneously ARE the world they need. The world is not something outside of the mongoose! A mongoose FEELS, EXPERIENCES the world. It experiences the cobra, it experiences the scent; it's all part of itself. So it doesn't need to "guess." . . . The bird flying from Siberia doesn't need to guess whether Ceylon is over there! Ceylon is not over there! At each instant, the world unfolds within the animal. And the moment it needs to be there, it's there. It isn't "over there," as it were. It isn't "tomorrow."

TOWARNICKI: *Yes, but man is not an animal!*

Well, he has cut himself off from everything; he has closed himself up in a glass bowl. He can no longer directly communicate with anything. He has to invent telephones, telexes, televisions or telescopes in order to communicate with what's over there.

But in the animal world there is no such a thing as "over there."

That's what we have trouble understanding.

The instinct of the bird is that it . . . IS the world. It IS geography. It IS Ceylon. It IS at every minute, wherever it flies; and at every minute, the entire world is present within it—the world unfolds inside it; it's not that it flies over the world.

> TOWARNICKI: *But, clearly, the animal cannot be a model for mankind?*

And why not?

This is precisely what we suffer most from: our inability to communicate with anything, to see anything clearly, to know anything. . . . We no longer know anything whatsoever! Except through books, committees, doctors, engineers, etc. Through that whole enormous apparatus, we manage to know a few things. But let's try removing . . . let's get rid of our machinery, and we no longer know anything of the world! We have no power over the world, no vision of the world, except for what's immediately under our nose.

> TOWARNICKI: *All right, but the scope of the bird or the animal is relatively limited. Man has a different station in the universe. He doesn't have that . . .*

Well, the day he regains that breadth of the animal, that total communication of the animal, coupled with the consciousness he has acquired, his range of action will not be as limited as a bird's or a mongoose's or a dog's. His range of action will be much greater.

Reincarnation (The Taxi Meter)

TOWARNICKI: *In an experience like Sri Aurobindo's or Mother's, or yours, what is the place for a belief in reincarnation?*

First of all, it isn't a belief. It's a fact.

But so much fantasy has been mixed with it that it's difficult to talk about.

Our technical and scientific civilization talks of atavism, of chromosomes, of grandfather and great grandfather—it's another way of talking about "reincarnation." But as always, we only grasp a very superficial aspect.

There is no doubt that a human being is not born into the world for the first time. Because, truly, if his human experience were limited to what he is for 40, 60 or 37 years of his life, it would be a frightening absurdity: to open one's eyes for so little experience and so little time. If really one keeled over at the end and that's it, it would be rather monstrous.

But we have such a limited and short vision of things.

Though we do feel, in our own flesh, that certain things in our life that are so burning, so painful or contradictory must come from somewhere else.

Why do some beings have a greater intensity about them than others? Why do some beings have a heavier darkness to bear? Why do some beings cry out for the Light?

Is it because of the chromosomes of a grandfather, a mother or a great grandfather? Or is it not, rather, the continuation of a question they raised a long time ago? Or a difficulty they confronted a long time ago, which they could not resolve? Or a call they uttered a long time ago, which is starting to get an answer?

Talking of this is very difficult because people immediately turn it into a soap opera, and they become the reincarnation of Alexander the Great or Charlemagne or . . . All that is utterly childish.

We are the reincarnation of our hope.

We are the reincarnation of our prayer.

We have yearned a lot, hoped a lot, prayed for something to be realized—well, it doesn't just end because you are put on a funeral pyre or into a hole. That prayer, that call, follows you . . . it follows you. Or that heavy darkness you experienced follows you.

If we could see the total picture, we would see the same story unfolding from one age to another, with different cloaks, different apparent circumstances. But behind all those appearances (whether in Egypt, Greece, Rome, Europe, India), behind that setting we would see the same constant seeking—the same crying out for something. And then, from time to time, in that setting, in those particular clothes, we would suddenly be seized and immobilized by such a profound breath—something that makes all clothing fall away, that puts us in a great, great lineage, on a great, great road, which has been forever, and then . . . we feel: I will be forever.

TOWARNICKI: *A beautiful, enchanting tale! But it is a realm without any certainty.*

Well, look, certainties are . . . During those few seconds when the clothing, the setting, falls away—that void in which everything seems to collapse like a house of cards—at that moment, it's so clear, you know, that there's no place for doubt, no place for certainties *(laughing)*: you're experiencing a fact.

You know that you've lived "that" before, and you'll live it again; that it is like the very essence of your being through its entire journey, in Roman, Greek, Egyptian or Hindu clothing, and it's one and the same BEING that went through that . . . course.

> **TOWARNICKI:** *Therefore it's a reincarnation of an individuality, a personality, a consciousness? That's what is the most difficult to grasp. Because many people believe in a sort of reincarnation of forces, even in the physical, biological sense. But the reincarnation of a consciousness, a personality, a "self"—this is more difficult to grasp, the more so since most people have no actual recollection of a past life.*

Naturally.

But what can actually be "carried over" from one life to another?

All our material preoccupations (whether in Greek, Egyptian, Hindu, Chinese or French), all our material preoccupations—"I'm going to make so much," "I'm going to get such and such a position," "I'm going to establish a family"—all that is a substance completely null, as it were. It doesn't remain. It changes, breaks up, dies.

But what does remain in a life?

Let's take our life, this one—what remains of it?

If we look back twenty or thirty years, if we take a bird's-eye view of this existence, what actually remains?

Is it all our material preoccupations and the thousands of futile things that come with them? No. But there are special moments when we are like a . . . like a pure cry, or like a wide vision opening up, perhaps on nothing—and yet it is the only thing existing.

Those moments SHINE.

They are the only thing that remains of the 20, 30 or 40 years of our existence.

All of a sudden, we stop on the street and look at the crowd—that meaningless crowd, that crowd of shadows rushing to their appointments, their subway, their deals— we stand there as if lost, a tiny point in the crowd, and a sort of cry bursts out of the depth of our heart. Our eyes open, and we say to ourselves, "But . . . but . . . who? Who am I? What am I? Who is this person in the middle of this crowd of shadows?"

At that moment a sort of vision opens up in us. Everything stops. The crowd disappears. All the vain things disappear. And there is such a very special kind of vibration in the heart. It's as if that second had always vibrated.

And suddenly that park bench in the evening light is as if imprinted forever, that shop window is imprinted forever— insignificant details are as if imprinted for eternity. And they are associated with that second when a cry suddenly burst out of us, when we suddenly uttered our true human cry.

That remains. Those are the true seconds in an entire life.

Those moments when we broke out of the theater of life, when we raised our "question," when our unique vision opened up, when the present second became full.

That's what remains.

That's what is carried over into another life.

And for many people, there have been very few seconds in their life. Others have had more of those rather burning and intense seconds.

This is perhaps what explains the difference of intensity among beings, or the difference of "quality."

There you have an inkling of what reincarnation might be.

It isn't the reincarnation of a great warrior or a great consul, you see. It is the reincarnation of a little flame of truth seeking more and more to fill this life so full of empty hours, so empty they seem never to have existed.

And they are beings who strive more and more to fill, to PACK that one minute with existence.

I remember being on the roads of Brazil; I remember walking. . . . And I would look at the pebbles on the road, saying to myself, "EACH SECOND, EACH PEBBLE MUST EXIST. Each second must have its own plenitude. It shouldn't be something on which I walk and walk and walk, and it's all nonexistent."

In a taxi in Paris, I watched the meter ticking away: 60 centimes, 80 centimes, 1 franc—and what was happening during ALL THAT TIME? A meter ticking away 20 more centimes, 40 more centimes. I looked at that meter, and I was . . . petrified. I said to myself, "But what IS during all this time? What is, which is not 20 centimes? What IS?"

Those are the seconds that remain. And when one begins to experience those seconds, they have such a "purity" about them, as it were, such a simple beauty. It's such a TRUE HUMAN CRY, you know, that you want them to happen again and again, that each second BE, be ALIVE; that you be what you really are: be a human being at each second. Not just a three-piece suit going from one subway station to another, from one deal to another, from one woman to another. . . . What is there in all that? It's all frightfully empty.

But those little seconds when we suddenly stop and a CRY bursts out: Where am I? Where am I? What am I doing? What am I DOING in all this?

And when that "question" becomes sufficiently intense or burning, it's as if it suddenly became the answer itself. As if, for once, you were something.

So those seconds live forever, as it were.

And from life to life each human being becomes increasingly "human" . . . increasingly "full" of what he really is.

Not a setting, not particular clothing, not a function, you see, not an addition to fill out a passport or a police file; but a few burning little seconds, so true and pure, when, all of a sudden, being a man has a meaning . . . which is not there in a fish or a stork.

> **TOWARNICKI:** *In India, the belief in reincarnation is still very common . . .*

But it isn't a—

> **TOWARNICKI:** *Is reincarnation, for you, the manner in which people live that belief? I mean, belief in reincarnation is very common in India; perhaps it was even invented, born here. Today it is still lived by millions and millions of Indians. Is it, for you, what is being lived in one manner or another?*

What I tried to explain is the thing in its essence, in its deeper truth.

But for an Indian, reincarnation is not a belief. I would say it isn't more a belief for them than chromosomes and atavism are a belief for us. It is a fact they regard as perfectly evident, because they feel it in their own flesh. They understand that when some misfortune strikes them, well, it must be the continuation of something that happened before. And when the misfortune happens, for them, it isn't an "accident"; it's a problem they have to solve, which they may not have solved in a previous life, and which now comes back. Well, better solve the accident now or it will come again.

The actual sense of reincarnation is that of a progress in the development of consciousness.

Difficulties come to us not as accidents, but to FORCE us to take one more step forward. Not to overwhelm us, but to FORCE us to walk.

If we could only see how positive EVERYTHING is. That there is never any accident, never any misfortune—never, EVER—even in what seems to be the most dreadful. That EVERYTHING has a positive sense, and EVERYTHING is a means to make us take one more step in the development of our being. And that, taken globally, history—of nations, of continents, of civilizations—is a means to make all this terrestrial consciousness take one more step.

For you can see reincarnation in history, too: from one continent to another, from one nation to another. And even in the history of a given nation.

What is absolutely ridiculous is the whole fantasy that's mixed with it. That's rubbish: "I was so and so," "I was a great general," "I was . . ." It doesn't make sense—not much, at least. It isn't always absolutely false, but in 99.9 percent of the cases it's pure fiction and imagination.

TOWARNICKI: *So this is in line with . . . in the perspective of evolution?*

But everything is evolution!
There's nothing but evolution!
And what evolution? Evolution of what?
What is evolution?

It's the discovery of the Beauty that is there, of the Love that is there—of THAT which is there, truly, right in front of our eyes, in matter, in ourselves, in our body.

It isn't the discovery of anything else really.

It is the discovery of what is there, which we don't see, which we don't understand—which is covered over by all sorts of habits.

It is, in fact, the gradual uncovering of a marvel.

Each species is like a new vision opening on the earth.

Our human vision obviously is more open than that of a mongoose. But it still isn't the "total" vision of what is THERE on earth.

Evolution is a growing vision.

And finally, it means being all that is there.